THE ACTOR

DON MIGUEL RUIZ
BARBARA EMRYS

The
Actor

How to Live an Authentic Life

Leaping Hare Press

Brimming with creative inspiration, how-to projects and useful information
to enrich your everyday life, Quarto Knows is a favourite destination for those
pursuing their interests and passions. Visit our site and dig deeper with our
books into your area of interest: Quarto Creates, Quarto Cooks, Quarto Homes,
Quarto Lives, Quarto Drives, Quarto Explores, Quarto Gifts, or Quarto Kids.

First published in the UK in 2021 by Leaping Hare,
an imprint of The Quarto Group.
The Old Brewery, 6 Blundell Street,
London, N7 9BH, United Kingdom.
www.QuartoKnows.com

A catalogue record for this book is available from the British Library.

ISBN 978-0-7112-6722-0
Ebook ISBN 978-0-7112-6723-7

1 2 3 4 5 6 7 8 9 10

Cover design by Georgie Hewitt
Typeset in Centaur MT

Printed and bound by CPI Group (UK) Ltd, Croydon, CR0 4YY

Contents

Orientation Day

Good morning, and welcome to your personal Mystery School!

This week we begin a series of teachings about your life from an artist's point of view. Since you were old enough to speak, you've told countless stories about your personal experiences. You've spent decades expressing your feelings and documenting your actions. And yet in many ways, you remain a mystery to yourself. We're here together now to investigate the most compelling mystery of all: you.

As this series expands, so will your awareness. You will discover more about your world, how it was created, and how it can be modified for your happiness. Your world is the reality you perceive. You may think people see things exactly as you do, and make the same assumptions about what they see, but everyone's world is unique. Your personal reality is a distinct work of art, shaped by your own ways of thinking and imagining.

These courses are intended to help you recognize the creative choices that have made your reality what it is now, and the choices that are still available to you.

Of course, you've walked this campus since you were born. You've attended many similar classes in your life and explored mysteries for longer than you can remember. You've attended many orientation days like this one, and many graduation ceremonies. You've been a student and you've been a teacher, sharing your wisdom with others as you move through life.

You, like every human, arrived on this planet without knowledge. You could see and sense, but you were intellectually blind. And like most new humans, you raised your little lamp—let's call it curiosity—and moved forward into the darkness. You were hungry for light and everything light could reveal.

As you solved each of life's mysteries, more mysteries revealed themselves. Revelations came faster as your awareness grew. Your questions became deeper and their answers more challenging to process. This has been the way with you since your life began.

There's an ancient story that exists in human imagination. It concerns a gathering of wise entities in the heavens. They decided to create a mystery school, and that school would be called Earth. There are many versions of this story, but most agree that it took a long time to prepare this school. Science tells us it took billions of years to create an environment that could sustain life on this planet. It took billions more to build a campus where artists could come and discover the mysteries of life. To put it another way, it took an extremely long process of evolution to bring us to this particular moment—where, together, we can discover a new way of understanding *you*.

Every bit of knowledge, every topic, is a new field of exploration. Many people like you have explored the sciences and became experts in their field. Some study philosophy and social sciences. Some become chemists, physicists, engineers. Some dedicate themselves to religion, or to the law. Some excel at sports and some excel at the arts. Some very inspired students go on to inspire all of humanity. You may be among them, and more like you will follow.

Today, mysteries are yielding to human curiosity faster than ever. For many years now, you've been a part of this global academy where mysteries are examined and secrets are revealed. You've been a student even before your traditional schooling began. By now you've shown the world your skills, and you have the ability to develop more. You have the power to improve the quality of your life every day.

You are mastering you, even now. Using the power of attention, you can continue to see more, realize more, and take charge of your level of awareness. As I'm sure you've observed by now, even masters never stop learning. You've mastered many skills, but you too have miles to go before the adventure is over.

Being a student of life is like entering a maze that contains countless paths, each of which offers more choices. As you wind your way through the maze, it's impossible to see where each turn will lead you. Your life evolves according to the paths you follow, and your decisions are affected by everyone you encounter on the journey. Other students have influenced your perception of yourself. Their reflections have already affected the trajectory of your life and will, in some way, shape your future.

Teachers provide insights, but students cannot see what they're not ready to see. Your work with me is also an artistic exchange. I use the clearest language I can when I speak, that is my artistic contribution. You listen attentively, at your own level of comprehension, that is your contribution. How I choose my words is my responsibility, and how you interpret my words is yours. Together we are creating awareness out of mystery.

During our time together, you will recall familiar secrets and you will also uncover many surprising ones. You will begin to see clearly where once you were disoriented or confused. The discoveries you make here will give power to the present moment and help you make peace with the past. I suggest you see even the smallest revelation as a lightning bolt to energize the next day's journey.

This Mystery School series will address the challenges you face as you continue to shape your world. In future classes, we will discuss your personal mythologies and the power they exert over every aspect of your life. We will discuss romantic relationships, and the many ways we bond as human beings. There are so many doorways to learning, but this week we begin with a review of the dramatic arts.

Why? Acting is our first learned skill—even before language, and even before we stand up to walk. Performance art is a way of life for every person, and it has influenced our common dream. You, for instance, are the main character in every story you've told about yourself, and your loyalty to that character often keeps you from realizing your authenticity as a human being.

This week you have the opportunity to see the human drama as a whole, as well as the role you play in it. You may notice many things you couldn't before. You may decide to modify your actions as a result. New discoveries help us see that we have choices in life. How we make those choices is up to us.

It's an interesting world; you are an interesting individual. Again, welcome! Lift your little lamp. Bring your excellent curiosity. Bring an enthusiasm for adventure, and always remember to open your mind to the truth.

Day 1:
The
Artist

The Actor

"...the artist can fashion a beautiful
thing; and if he does not do it solely for
his own pleasure, he is not an artist at all."

–Oscar Wilde

A good day to you! Today, we begin our course in dramatic arts. In this particular school, every topic is meant to improve your understanding of human thinking and behavior. Every lesson brings you a step closer to wisdom and awareness. How you listen is up to you. How you apply each lesson is for you to decide.

There are some students who go to school anxious to learn. Maybe you've been that kind of student in the past. There are some who go to school but get easily distracted. That also could be you. There are some who fail to take notes or remember what they've learned. And there are some who show up, attend a few classes, and drop out early. Dropping out indicates a mysterious lack of interest. If you were that kind of student, you probably wouldn't be here now.

No, I suspect you've been interested in solving life's mysteries since you arrived on campus, but you've entered a new level of discovery now. So leave your old

19

ideas at the door. Settle in, listen, and prepare to see with different eyes. With an open mind and a willingness to experiment, you can turn abstract ideas into observable actions.

Good! We've gone through the introductions, so let's begin this class by speaking about the artist. Before any work of art can be created, there must first be an artist. Energy, you can say, is the artist of the natural world. You are the artist of your own reality. The impulse to create is in your genetic makeup. You were born to it.

What defines an artist, exactly? Well, many things. An artist has an eye for beauty. An artist looks for wonder in the physical world *and* the virtual world. An artist sees what isn't readily seen by others, and shares that vision with humanity. An artist knows how to surrender to the creative force...to be thoughtless and in love.

Some of those definitions might not seem familiar to you. They might seem a little eccentric. Eccentricity is considered a characteristic of artists, but aren't we all eccentric and strange? You may not like the way some people express their art, but every expression has a right to exist. We are all artists, and our talents are diverse and remarkable. You and I are architects, painters, and storytellers, just for a start. There's no need to argue over technique and style, because we each do it according to our instincts. Every artist processes information in a unique way.

We do our best with the tools at hand, which include the brain we were born with and the knowledge we've accumulated. Given inferior tools, a sculptor might produce inferior work. Given only a small amount of light, or very few colors, any painter would be challenged. And yet, challenges often lead to exciting and innovative art. Genius lies in the distinctive expression of every individual, whatever the restrictions.

Before we discuss the nature of your talents, let's talk about nature itself. Let's talk about the emergence of the artist into the physical realm. You and I were born into a world that can legitimately be called a masterpiece of art. You can see that, surely. Earth is a perfect creation. It took billions of years for this planet to evolve into the marvel it is. We, too, are a marvel. Humanity is new by comparison, but it has experienced its own astonishing evolution. And the process continues, for both the planet and the species. Every one of us is a transforming work of art.

You, the Marvel

We all began life as authentic beings, but authenticity became elusive as we grew into adulthood. Authenticity got lost in the relentless song and dance, you could say. We learned to live up to other peoples' expectations of us. We learned to pretend, and to be blind to the pretense. In the human drama, truth is often forgotten for the sake of the show. But, deep within the spectacle, truth waits to be illuminated. Underneath all the theatrics, truth is what we are.

Like everyone else, you were conceived by wondrous means and made into a human within a few short months. Everyone develops according to life's biological blueprint. Energy is the architect, the artist. Energy makes matter and directs the evolution of matter. You were conceived, born, and refined into a work of perfection by energy's unstoppable force.

At the moment of your conception, you started your education. Even in the womb, you approached the mysteries of being human one puzzle at a time. Life has been your teacher, guiding you from your earliest moments. When you broke the physical connection with your biological mother, you started to learn from the rest of humanity. As your infant brain matured, it began to define your personal universe. It learned to recognize sounds, shapes, faces. At a certain point, someone spoke your name and you recognized it as your own. Someone hooked your attention, which began the formal process of learning. You imitated their words, and were on your way to mastering a language.

At first you didn't know what you knew or didn't know—and you didn't care. Why should you? You were born not understanding what you saw or heard, but you were destined to figure it out. Slowly, you learned to distinguish one thing from another. You singled out emotions and gave a kind of order to the chaos. Step-by-step, unknowns become known. As your nervous system evolved, you became adept at solving mystery after mystery.

The mind of every artist is created from bits of knowledge and memory. Your mind developed according to the stories you heard and the ideas you accepted as true. Meanwhile, your body continued to be guided by life's energy.

At four or five years of age, you went to your first mystery school away from home. Perhaps it was nursery school, or kindergarten, where you learned the rules of human conduct from other people. You studied the social arts, where "getting along" and "fitting in" meant everything. You were taught to share and to play nice. You received constant reminders: *Don't kick! Don't bite! Use your inside voice! Wait your turn!* These techniques helped you become an artist of diplomacy in a world of contrasting cultures.

In first grade, you were taught to read, to write, and to work with numbers. To a small child, these are staggering mysteries—until they're not. After a time of struggle and discipline, you began to break the codes. You became a kind of magician, revealing the unseen and discovering the unexpected. A handful of letters suddenly became sentence, a thought, a story—a universe.

And numbers! The symbols 0-9 introduced amazing games, mathematical solutions, and entirely new universes. At first, numbers could only be managed on the fingers of two little hands. As your brain grew in complexity, so did the problem-solving power of numbers. From ten little fingers, your calculations took you all the way to the infinite! How could you have imagined such things when your studies began?

In those early years, you also fell in love with music. Just twelve tones, you found, could create an infinite library of sounds. There's that word again: *infinite.*

Infinite... Limitless... Never ending. All symbols yield to it eventually. In fact, the more we understand about ourselves, the more likely we are to find ourselves at the doorstep of infinite mystery.

In elementary school you studied simple science, where experiments revealed some of life's basic secrets. You began to learn about the physical world a little at a time. You began to understand your place in it, and your relationship to all living things. You did all of this—adding, multiplying, reading, singing, experimenting—not knowing you were training to be a master. Then, as now, you were the artist, and life was your creative partner.

Then came middle school, where more complex mysteries become familiar. You were also rocked by the secrets of your own body. Puberty! Physical changes meant emotional changes—and even deeper mysteries. And that adventure hasn't ended. Your body continues to change in dynamic ways. You'll make adjustments to the changes, even into old age, but the body's mysteries, like the mysteries of the universe, will puzzle and intrigue you for a lifetime.

After middle school came high school, then college, perhaps, and then a job and career. Every new school, every profession, represented a different culture. Each demanded that you learn a new dialect and break new codes. They required you to reimagine yourself, and adapt to bigger changes.

Can you recall any of that now? Change leads to more change, so you may never have recognized how much you transformed in a short time. Here on Earth is where you learned and you matured. Here, you developed free will and began to make decisions according to your own philosophies. You gathered information and experience on this campus, until you, too, became a master and a teacher. Whatever your age, you're still transforming.

Your library of knowledge is your alma mater. What you say and what you think are the laws you live by. Right or wrong, your mind—with all its views and opinions—runs the show. The mind creates a version (or, more accurately, a distortion) of the real universe. It observes what is, and makes sense of everything in its own artistic way. It recreates what has already been created by life. It copies. It reinvents. As a result, we humans build tunnels, towers, and bridges as they exist in nature. We duplicate nature, and in some ways we improve on it.

Over the centuries, we've learned to unlock the basic mysteries of physics and to reconstruct matter. And we've gone farther, we've challenged the elements. We've defied gravity. We've dared to fly—even to hurl ourselves into space. We're adventurers, explorers, and accomplished sorcerers. We are artists, and our strange art affects every species on Earth.

There are many kinds of artists attending this university. Some sculpt objects out of clay and stone. Some bend metals, carve wood, weave fabric. Some artists write, and reveal the human condition through their words. Artists fashion things out of imagination. They construct, they dream, they invent. And no matter their particular expertise, artists have one thing in common: they act, they emote, they perform. They practice the art of dramatic interpretation—which leads us to our topic of the week.

The Actor

This class is focused on a specific kind of art, one that has kept humanity enthralled for thousands of years: acting. We'll discuss acting in more depth later in the week, but let's take a quick look now at how it relates to you and to your reality.

We are all players and spectators in the human drama—that includes you. You are the experienced actor, having gone through years of training without ever realizing it. You are a thespian. You're also a fan of the theater. We are all enthusiastic supporters of the arts, and we all have specific performing talents of our own, although those talents may not be recognizable to us, or to anyone.

Acting is mostly reacting. We're always in reaction, and there are many ways to react. Just as an actor makes different choices in a scene, you and I choose our favorite reactions. Say I poke you with my elbow a little too energetically. You can react with anger and pretend to be injured. Or you can laugh. Or you can give me a hug. Or you can do nothing, which is also a reaction.

Reacting is an artistic choice, not just a strategic one. You've been studying this art for a lifetime. By now, you favor certain reactions over others. You may even feel those reactions define you. Performing is a learned skill. You picked it up even before you mastered a vocabulary. Before you learned the words, you'd already mastered the attitudes. Before you found out that there's such a thing as filmmaking, you were the star of your own movie, dramatizing your words and actions.

As kids, most of us developed a hunger for audience response—something we never really got over. Realizing our own talent for drama, we dedicated ourselves to the craft, conditioning our bodies to react to the slightest offense, the smallest worry. Even moody silences are dramatic reactions. Pouting is a performance. For some actors, it's a trademark skill. And all such skills begin early in life.

You began your training soon after birth, imitating the actors who came before you. You did this for survival—and for fun. Back then, your audience was programmed to love everything you did. You smiled, and they laughed. You burped, and they cheered. You babbled incoherently, and they clapped. The amount of pleasure it gave people to see you try to walk—and start to talk—is impossible to measure. You were a hit with everyone. In no time, you were taking your act on the road, make-believing with your little friends, switching roles, changing plots. Without knowing it, you were practicing for the role of your life, in the longest running play ever to hit the stage.

Of course, as your performance lost its freshness and spontaneity, your fan base got smaller. Inevitably, you began to remind everyone of everyone else. After a while, the laughter seemed forced and the cheers were muted. Even so, you played on, adapting your act to the needs of the moment and the expectations of the crowd. You were a trouper, and still are.

As any professional actor will tell you, it's important to deliver a compelling performance, no matter how an audience responds. Commit to doing your best, whether they're with you or not. An audience may be restless and noisy, or composed of just a few people. They may not laugh when they should or be shocked when you want them to be. It shouldn't matter. You're not playing for them, you're playing for you.

In this world there are hundreds, thousands, and millions of *them*. The world is teeming with critics. They're all followers of something. They're devoted to soccer, astrology, fashion, food. And fans have their own tastes and preferences. How can you know what an audience wants? How can you hope to please everyone?

"Tuning out" the audience is a challenge to most performers—after all, artists were trained to please. Their happiness has always relied on a positive response from someone else. The things that frighten most professional actors are the same things that frighten the amateur—meaning you, me, and the rest of humanity. They're afraid to be judged.

We all take the risk of being judged on a daily basis. We step out of the house each morning to face a world full of critics. All the world is a stage—and you are only one of several billion players. Fortunately, most of them are too busy judging their own performance to notice yours.

Professional actors, on the other hand, must step into the lights and be scrutinized by those who have come specifically to judge them. They're examined by faceless people sitting in the dark, people whose expectations are high and whose judgments are often ruthless. Actors are panned by unseen critics and adored by nameless fans. Bad press can break them emotionally. It has, on occasion, almost broken you, hasn't it?

The judgments of your peers have hurt you in the past. So you already understand the trials of an artist very well. The fear of being judged is a handicap we all share, whatever our talents. It makes it hard for us to walk onto a stage or into the workplace. It's scary to step into the lights with other skilled artists, any of whom may be more talented or more attractive. If that isn't enough, consider what else professional actors have to worry about.

To create effective drama, actors must imagine, and remember. They must have faith in what they do. Faith means believing in something one hundred percent, and a good story is only as good as our ability to believe it. So actors believe. We all believe. We believe what we say, and hope that our audience believes us, too. We put real emotion into our performances, so that our bodies don't always know the difference between an act and an actual experience.

We've all felt the pain of regret. We've lived the horror of a trauma over and over again. Old wounds come to life when we summon them. Memory can work against us, but that hasn't kept us from bringing the past to mind often, regardless of the pain it causes. This is a practiced art.

Professional actors call on intimate and disturbing memories from their own lives in order to make a scene believable. They often recreate moments of trauma to inform their art. They act out emotions so well that audiences become engrossed, and sometimes even uncomfortable. Stage actors do these eight performances a week for months at a time. That sounds like a lot. On the other hand, the rest of humanity is doing it non-stop.

Eight performances a week (including matinees) is nothing for most people. It's probably nothing for you. Don't you repeat your favorite narratives over and over, to the discomfort of everyone around you? Don't you lie awake at night, without an audience, and relive the worst moments of the day? Most of us imagine future failures. How about you? Do you fear what tomorrow will bring? Do worst-case scenarios run through your mind all day? Do you believe what you fear? The greater the actor's belief, the more intense the audience's response—even when the audience is only you, listening to yourself in the dark.

The job of every actor is difficult enough—just having to learn the lines, commit them to memory, and deliver them convincingly. On top of that, they deal with technical problems and unpredictable audiences. They miss cues and stumble over furniture. Just like the rest of us, they often fail at the thing they're most passionate about doing well.

Maybe the biggest challenge for a professional actor is returning to the world offstage. When the play is over, it's important for an actor to recover emotional balance. Once the theater goes dark, performers must find themselves again. This goes for all of us. Every day, artists—plumbers, politicians, teachers (and you)—push their bodies to emotional limits. You say you can't help it, that you are a passionate person, but passion and drama are different things. Passion is truth, drama is theater. It's a good time in your evolution to see the difference, and to choose.

It's hard to walk away from an intensely dramatic scene. It takes a while to find some inner calm after a fight. When tempers flare and our defenses are activated, most of us react automatically. Habits take charge, so we say things we usually say when we're afraid and angry. We recite the usual lines. Our body language is already programmed, so we kick things, break things, or slam a door. We put on a predictable show. We are seasoned actors following old scripts. "I don't know why I say that stuff," we may reflect afterward, but the next performance is the same. So, too, are the apologies and justifications.

You're capable of doing more than following old stage directions. You can rewrite the script. You can also improvise. Experience informs the things you say and the choices you make, but so does imagination.

So does ingenuity. Every production deserves a fresh interpretation, every actor yearns for a new approach. You, the artist, can do this; you can expand your talents and renew your passions. You can pursue truth through your art.

As you developed as an artist, you learned a lot about yourself. You learned your strengths and weaknesses, your talents and terrors. From the days of being afraid of the dark, you learned to fortify your defenses. You learned to accept judgments, or fight back. You learned to run from conflict, or to face it. Along the way, you've collected a stash of secrets, as everyone does. The secrets you keep—especially from yourself—will likely create more fear. Enough fear, and you're unable to perform on any stage.

If you're afraid to hold your little lamp up to the truth, you'll remain an enigma to yourself: the mystery you're least willing to solve. Childhood fears fall away, but grown-up fears last a lifetime if they're not confronted. What you're able to see in yourself you're able to see in everyone. And *seeing* is the essence of art. A blind artist still has vision. It's important that artists study themselves. It's important that you do. "What will I find then?" you may ask. "What monsters must I face? How can I possibly fight back against the truth?"

Knowing yourself intimately is never the nightmare you expect, far from it. Knowing yourself breathes new life into a love affair that began in childhood. Look away, and the affair will end swiftly. Feeling genuine love for yourself is a homecoming. It's a return to paradise. And paradise is a great place to improve your art.

Why Does Any of This Matter?

You've already mastered so many aspects of the performing arts. You may now consciously turn your attention to mastering the art of being an authentic human. Sound impossible? Not really.

You've come to this kind of turning point before. Your first attempts to walk led to failure. You stumbled and fell, but were so determined to work at it, to improve your craft, that nothing could discourage you. Eventually, you learned to move with balance and confidence. Maybe you mastered some athletic skills. You also excelled in the arts of speech and emotional drama. Every mastery improved your life and expanded your awareness.

Practicing any art develops the brain. The more agile the brain, the easier it is to learn anything. Children who study dance, music, painting, or acting have an academic advantage. They also have the rare ability to abandon thought and surrender to the creative impulse, a talent that serves them in every aspect of life.

What does it matter, to know yourself as an artist? The artist recognizes that each of us is a universe living within countless universes. With an artist's eye, you can appreciate colors, shapes, and the vibrations of life. Secret by secret, you can reveal yourself, just as you would the mysteries of the moon, the stars, the sun, and the Earth. Piece by piece, you begin to see the whole picture.

The artist's eye searches for beauty. Beauty is the grace that moves you through the world. Beauty is the gratitude you feel when you're truly inspired. Beauty lies in a well-chosen phrase, the gift of a smile, and the respect one person shows another. Every living form possesses its own kind of beauty. Every physical body is a work of art.

Your mind is a glass-blower, shaping a delicate world for your body to occupy. It matters that you make that world transparent and pleasing to the eye.

It matters that you make it a dream of beauty and purpose, from which others can drink inspiration. And let's not forget your most artistic gift: the genius of words.

It's no small thing to become familiar with the language you speak, a language unique to you. You have your own way of using words, either to inspire or to do harm. You choose the mood and the tone behind the syllables you speak. It's never too late to recognize the voice in your head, always prompting, always predicting. That voice is yours. No one else controls it.

Listen closely to its repetitive messages. Do they represent who you are, or how you want to sound? Maybe the voice you're hearing once belonged to someone else, someone you tried hard to impersonate or to please. Maybe it belonged to the character you used to play. Maybe you're too old now to play past roles, or too wise. You can let them go any time. You can pack away the old costumes and ignore the echo of past monologues in your head. If you choose, you can simply *be*.

How Do I Begin?

Would it be weird to move through society without a role to play? It might feel like going onto a battlefield unarmed. It may seem strange at first just to observe and enjoy, to ignore old impulses and reactions, and just listen. Listening is a big challenge, even to a seasoned actor, but it reveals answers to many mysteries. You can learn fascinating things about other artists. You might learn to understand your species. You will definitely learn more about yourself.

Listen. Observe. Trust life, in all its whimsy. Find ways to express yourself more fully. Use your own voice to sing life's music and to speak its language. Go your own way, while respecting the ways of others. Set aside your defenses and laugh at your fears.

Instead of echoing everyone else, you can nurture your individuality and spontaneity. Accept situations as they present themselves, and respond honestly. Maybe you do that already. Do you welcome the unexpected? Can you manage disappointment with grace? If not, make these your new disciplines.

Broaden your interpretation of the roles you play. You've created a character to present to the world, and in some ways, you've allowed that character to develop subtle shades and adaptable traits. In other ways, you've lost flexibility; certain traits have become rigid and uncompromising. Instead of developing a taste for beauty and a talent for love, you've sometimes been guarded and suspicious. At times, you've neglected those you love. And too often, you've neglected your most precious ally: your own body.

The body is its own work of art. You might think it to be large, bulky, or slow. It may seem skinny or feeble, but still it can be guided with confidence and style. How do you walk into a room? Are you expecting rejection or commanding interest? Observe, and be willing to make changes. If not for the body, you'd have no chance to participate in the human spectacle. You'd have no opportunity to exhibit your art in any form.

Professional actors usually go through years of training. They're mindful of how they move. They learn to dance. They work out. Since an actor's voice is so vital to the craft, they take care of it. They're taught to project when they speak, and to breathe efficiently. They take singing lessons. They practice tonal exercises and tongue-twisters. They keep their tools in good working condition.

Like any actor, your body is your essential instrument. It's an exceptional work of art, but it can also generate art. Without the body, there's no actor and there's no performance. Your body meets the world for you. It plays the tune you want to share. It tells the stories you want to tell. It produces emotions and conjures words. It fights, it seduces—and, absolutely, it creates. Your body creates life and many replications of life. It turns little ideas into things of beauty and power.

So your education as an artist begins with attention to the body. The most basic question you can ask yourself is, "How can I take better care of it?" You probably don't treat your body like the precious instrument it is. More likely, you take it for granted. It's doubtful you take the time to thank your body, or give it an occasional caress. It's unlikely you even think about your brain, its most intricate organ and the hub of all your creativity.

What can you do? You can enhance ordinary moments by giving your body attention. Give it the encouragement it needs—that means talking, but also touching. Let it know how appreciated it is. Cherish your physical being as a classical violinist might cherish a Stradivarius. Your body is your most intimate partner. As with any good partnership, each is responsible for the welfare of the other.

Artists reflect life, and life is evident in everything seen and heard. Miss nothing. Judge nothing. Be open and accepting of it all. Alter the way you see the world. Allow small things to make an impression. Notice the endearing traits of a stranger. See an old friend with new eyes. Remark on the wonders of nature.

Learn to see from every point of view. Use perspective, every artist's secret tool. Be aware of it, along with your body, your brain, your voice. And don't forget how you choose your *words*.

Day 2:
Language

"When I use a word,' Humpty Dumpty
said in rather a scornful tone, 'it means
just what I choose it to mean, neither
more nor less.'"

—Lewis Carroll

Good morning! I hope you slept well, and that your
dreams were helpful to the learning process! Even now,
in the brilliance of the morning, you are dreaming. You
are imagining and interpreting. As the sound of my
words reaches your ears, you assume their meaning.
"Okay, I get it," you might say, and go to the next thing.
Instead, imagine how their meaning applies to your life.
Imagine reacting to situations in uncharacteristic ways
because you dreamed about my words in a new way.

By picturing yourself doing just one thing differently, or seeing just one thing in a way you never thought
of before, you change a little. You evolve. You expand
your usual perspective and you create a slightly different
reality for yourself, just as great artists do. You may not
see yourself as an artist, and yet your objective is to
create. You see things your way, and share that unique
perception through your art.

Everyone is destined to create a story, for instance. You create stories, and you always have. At an early age, you learned to give names to everything. You were trained to apply all your experiences to the development of your story. You were told who you were and who your ancestors were. You were given a history, and also a dream of the future. You were told all sorts of stories, and soon became your own storyteller.

Your personal story developed over time, inspiring every possible emotional reaction—joy, despair, and everything in-between. It's a story about the artist, told by the artist. You're at the center of a universe you create. Your story is different from every other story, but, as I'm sure you've noticed, all stories have important elements in common.

All stories have a protagonist—a character through whose eyes the reader sees the world. You've created such a character for yourself, and share his or her point of view with everyone who will listen. All stories have heroes and villains. Yours does, I'm sure. All stories appeal to people's emotions. You've probably noticed that your stories get a better response when you exaggerate the drama a little. Of course, none of this matters unless you and your listeners speak the same language.

What good is a story, however dramatic, if the words make no sense to the listener?

Students on the world campus speak many different languages. They speak the language their parents taught them in early childhood, and they also learn to speak the language of their chosen art. Many choose to learn the language of other artists and other cultures. Whether or not they see themselves as teachers, every artist will eventually teach others. Whether or not they see themselves as artists, they have been creating a masterpiece since they arrived.

Without language, you and I would have problems communicating effectively. Of course, we could scratch shapes in the dirt or paint on walls. We might gesture and point. Inevitably, we would have to work out a system of sounds, and those sounds would become more elaborate over time. As our speaking skills developed, we'd look for ways to explore more abstract ideas. We'd try to communicate feelings. We'd want to explain things that can't be seen.

That's the way language began for our species. We incorporated one sound, then another and another, according to mutual agreements. A language is built on agreements. You and I decide that this sound means this thing, and so on. That is the way language works, even now. If you think a word means something specific, and I interpret it another way, our communication fails. Disagreement leads to misunderstanding, and even the simplest misunderstanding can lead to the end of all communication.

When we agree on the meaning of words, when we enjoy listening to each other and sharing ideas joyfully, our communication improves. We develop our artistic skills. Language is an amazing, living form of art. Humans may not be the only species that practices this art, but we are masterful at it. It would be impossible to count the number of languages humanity has developed since its beginning, when men and women drew things in the dirt and painted animals on cavern walls.

How did you and I learn to speak the language of our people? We arrived as helpless infants, with no language skills beyond wordless screams and kicking feet. As our brains developed, we learned to distinguish sounds. Slowly, steadily, we began to interpret sounds and eventually mimic them. It happened over time, but it happened easily and organically. We were destined to be artists of words.

You know the role mimicking plays in childhood development. As a toddler, you heard the sounds that your parents and siblings made and you attempted to duplicate those sounds, syllable by syllable. You also observed actions and mannerisms. With a lot of practice and repetition, the baby eventually became the master.

The first thing you must have noticed in your infancy is how people talk and talk. They talk about themselves and they gossip about each other. In fact, gossip is the common tongue of humanity. Adults gossip, and children listen. They catch on quickly. Soon, they're gossiping with their peers and making fun of kids who aren't like them. This process, too, is easy and organic. As they watch their parents interact socially, children learn a subtle emotional language as well.

People tend to react emotionally (yes, even dramatically) to what they hear and see. Words of disapproval trigger hurt feelings, and people show it. Words of praise give pleasure, and they show that. They also act out their disappointment, indignation, and outrage. They're good at this, they've been practicing all their lives. People make faces. They yell and shout. They argue, and then, feeling remorse, they make up.

These are features of their art. Children learn these skills from experts.

Joy has its own expression. So does anxiety. So does heartbreak. The human body speaks a multitude of languages, which kids pick up at an early age. They notice and they imitate. They observe, learn, and bring their unique style to the craft. Technique, genius, and personal style: these are the qualities of a great artist. And you are definitely one. You and I show different kinds of genius, but we are both masters at being *who we say we are.*

Whatever your vocation, you probably sound like your peers. If you changed careers, you might sound a little different—because every professional speaks a different dialect. Doctors don't sound like dairy farmers. Attorneys don't sound like baristas. Each trade is its own culture. Changing locations changes the conversation. When you move around the country, you hear unfamiliar idioms. Beyond your country's borders, language and culture change. Those changes are enough to alter your reality.

Imagine humanity as a big herb garden, with a wide variety of plants that offer a wide variety of benefits. There are herbs that comfort, or cure, or agitate, but all plants function in similar ways. They require the same basic elements to exist. So do we. But while humans function in the same way as most living things, they also talk. They use symbols—printed words, sounds, and physical gestures—to communicate. Language is not only a necessary part of human survival, language is our astonishing art.

Breaking the Code

Humans use codes, or specific sets of symbols, to communicate. An alphabet is such a code. Countless words can be created out of just a few symbols, this is the wonder of language. Transferring an idea or a feeling into a few spoken syllables is a mystifying art. How the brain makes that happen is a matter for another mystery school, but for now let's discuss the codes we deciphered long ago.

All variations of our Latin alphabet consist of up to twenty-six letters, beginning with a, b, c. Mix these up, and you have a living language, subtle and adaptable—and proven to endure through the ages. The formula is the same in every culture: A handful of symbols, when rearranged, can produce countless phrases, making human communication as powerful and complex as it is.

And then there is the language of numbers. Counting zero, there are only ten symbols in this code—so few, and yet their ability to calculate and to quantify is limitless. Mathematical formulas provide solutions to life's biggest puzzles. Math has allowed humanity to build cities and empires. It has helped to cure disease and launch us into space. I and 0 have defined the computer age, altering communication forever. Numbers offer more ways to tell a story and to unravel life's most confounding mysteries.

Music, too, is a language of its own. Twelve notes, or tones, can be arranged in infinite ways to produce countless musical phrases. We can capture a tune, record it, and play it back as many times as we want, to our constant delight. Yes, music is a delight to the senses. Musical beats pulse through all matter. From the time of primitive humans, music has had the power to excite emotions and unsettle societies. It has defined our present values and documented our history.

I've mentioned three basic codes: words, music, numbers. Call them a-b-c, 1-2-3, and do-re-mi. All three work together in a mix of math and emotion. Without mathematics—the steady count of beats per phrase—there is no melody. Without words, melody can't tell a good story. Someone's passion is being sung in every poem, and every conversation carries a tune. And all of this adds up to performance art.

We perform with skill and awareness, or we do not. We put words to just the right music, but we can also seem tone-deaf. We behave like amateurs, and then we'll act with artistic precision. Art is subjective, personal, and always changing.

We create beauty out of words. We create books, plays, films, and lasting attachments with words. Words can inspire us to appreciate beauty if we've never been encouraged to do so before. Words excite. Words comfort. Like any artistic expression, words can also create divisions. Words can produce fear and animosity.

We have a curious relationship with symbols, it seems. We use them to our advantage and to our detriment...but we're not very good at seeing the difference. We're not great at breaking our own emotional codes.

Consider the role you play. How does your character use words to communicate with other characters? How does your character communicate with itself? Do your words support a negative viewpoint? Do they criticize, complain, and sometimes even mock the speaker?

You may think you sound positive and tolerant, but listen to your thoughts, they might not sound charitable. You think you are a cheerful person, but your frown says something else. You might swear you're an affectionate person, but your body language says you're not. You lean away from people. You avoid direct contact and warm gestures. I'm not accusing you, these are examples of how we all fool ourselves. Our self-image is often at odds with our own words and actions.

The body speaks its own language. It tells secrets that the mind is unwilling to disclose. Our moods and gestures deliver messages in spite of us, and they often speak more eloquently than words. Your face is "talking" whether or not you make a sound. Feeling disapproval, your mouth tightens. Your brows lift. Your arms cross in response to an unspoken threat. Your fists clench. Your shoulders rise and fall in silent judgment and your knees bounce with impatience. Your head tilts, turns, or ducks away from possible controversy. Who needs a voice when the rest of you is so emotionally transparent?

Most people keep their thoughts contained, but that doesn't mean their emotions aren't easily recognized—and transferred. In a play, an actor gives us an interpretation of a character's motives. Any audience can understand that language. In a book, a character's thoughts and feelings are written in detail, the reader gets it. Consider the art that is going on around you. Everybody is delivering a silent soliloquy. They're performing without speaking. Their faces offer clues. Their mental narrative is unknown to you, but you get the message anyway.

Emotion runs under the surface—it's chemical, subtle, but easier to interpret than speech. And it has a magnetic pull. We are naturally drawn toward another person's emotional drama. And we're not above pulling people into our own drama. Everyone likes a good story, and people who make stories come alive are charismatic. They can move crowds. Audiences want to feel, and they want their feelings to be mirrored. They want someone to feel as bad, or perhaps worse, than they do. They want a dose of drama, and a taste of the emotional food they remember from childhood.

Do you see it? Can you appreciate what you do— what we've all been taught to do? What you can see, you can change. And personal transformation begins with the smallest changes. You have time to improve your art while you walk this campus, so take advantage of every opportunity. Look closer. Listen more carefully. There are still so many mysteries left to solve.

Of course, you've learned a lot about yourself already. You've recognized your own artistic prowess by now, surely. How you think, how you speak, how you use words—and, yes, how you move your body—are all under your control. Right? Nobody writes material for you anymore. Nobody feeds you lines from the wings. Nobody tells you to smirk, to shrug, or to roll your eyes. You make these choices now...or do you?

Your behavior is so automatic that you may not notice most of what you do and say. You may not even be curious about it. You've learned your responses by heart the way you once memorized popular songs and multiplication tables. And now, maybe those responses rule you. Maybe language has betrayed you. Maybe words jump out of your mouth without warning and cause all kinds of problems. If so, what happened? Did the artist become lazy? Did the musician give up?

When was the last time you listened to yourself and questioned what you were saying? How often do you make a fresh observation—or say nothing, rather than saying something predictable? Do you dare correct yourself, or admit you have no idea what you're talking about? Have you ever tried to stop a runaway train of thought? Or, even better, have you ever tried to keep that train from leaving the station?

Outside opinions shouldn't control your thinking. Pay attention, and you can change the way you react. You can discard a few outdated beliefs. You can curb the monologues running inside your head. You can have pleasant *and* unpleasant experiences and remain emotionally stable.

As you make your way around campus, you can teach your mind a few new tricks. The mind is meant to be flexible, it can quit stubborn habits and yield to new ideas. Encourage it to laugh at itself. Allow it to appreciate beauty and to respect all things. Stop your fears from gaining momentum.

This is not about becoming a more adept actor; it's about becoming a better human being. It's about clearing away some mental fog and giving yourself more opportunities to see. And what you see, you can change.

Too Many Auditions

In order to get an acting job, you need to audition for a specific role. You're given a script and you're asked to perform a scene in an uncomfortable setting. It may seem that you've spent your life auditioning like this. And it might feel that you've spent significant amounts of time preparing for your next role.

You've moved from one social circle to another since your earliest days. Remember? Each situation was kind of a test, a way to exhibit your talents. Each new circumstance required you to please someone, or to resolve personal conflicts. Every new society was its own mystery school.

As you graduated from one school and enrolled in another, different rules applied. With every change, you were expected to get along with new people and to learn their language. Good communication may have grown more challenging, but its rewards were greater.

At its core, communication reflects a need for truth. You, like everyone, hope to be understood and to make real connections with people. You want your words to be faithful messengers of your intent, but they often fail. Words are symbols, they can only do so much to describe what exists. They suggest. They imply. Words pretend to be real things—but, as you've learned, they often do a better job of masking the truth than revealing it.

You know people who hide behind a wall of words. You, too, know how to use language to mislead and deceive. You recite lines. You deny and exaggerate. Telling lies often seems like the best method of dealing with people. In the past, lies may have defended you from bullies. They defended you from the hard truth, and they provided alibis when you were afraid. But what about the future? How much longer can lies really serve you?

You shouldn't have to audition for life. There is no need to fear the judgements of your peers. The friends you encounter on your strolls around campus are preoccupied with their own fears. They're concerned with fitting in, just as you are. Like you, they look for brave and authentic people to associate with, so it shouldn't be surprising that some of them have chosen you. Be aware, however, of the energy you spend trying to be them.

We are all capable of inspiring others. We are innovators. We are artists. We are storytellers and weavers of dreams. We like to solve silly riddles and explore profound mysteries. Wherever we come from, we go about our everyday business in the same way. A woman speaking Kirundi in an African market says the same kinds of things that women say in markets around the globe. She bargains for fresh produce in the morning. She gossips about the neighbor's family. She scolds her children when they misbehave and comforts them when they're sick. When night falls, she whispers words of desire to her husband. She understands the vocabulary of love, and how to put her needs into language.

All of us have things in common, but we come into the world as individuals. We approach every challenge differently, and with a style that is our own. We walk across our little stage with a singular stride. We speak with a voice that distinguishes us from other artists. The world celebrates those who are unafraid to be one of a kind.

Your gift to humanity is to remain genuine and unaffected. Your most valuable contribution is your authenticity. Your finest pursuit is the truth, as you walk through a market, across a campus, or onto any stage.

Why Does Any of this Matter?

Once again, you may be wondering, "What difference does all of this make to me?" Well, as a student of art, you want to make exciting choices. You want all your creative efforts to reveal some level of truth. The tools you need are close at hand: your body, your words, your voice. The quality of your art depends on how you apply those tools. Your happiness depends on the way your art reflects your vision.

Today, we focused on the art of the spoken word. How do you choose words? Do you say what you mean and mean what you say? Words are the tools of your trade. Are they obeying your intentions? If not, decide how they can serve you better. You utter the words and choose the tone. Are you paying attention to that process? Do you monitor your thoughts, or do they run ahead of you? You can improve your relationship with words by selecting them consciously and creatively.

An actor interprets symbols and brings words to life. We all do it. We interpret symbols. We say words in a way that suggests how we feel. Words are just words— they're dead things that come alive through imagination. Spoken with intent, words can move hearts and change minds. Your words—spoken or unspoken— have the power to change you. Just as they've fixed you to one role, they can open you and expand your vision of yourself.

Too often, words just fill the silences. You don't need to repeat mindless phrases, or to say the same things in the same ways as if you'd memorized the script. You can be a better communicator by listening, and making sure your words represent who you are now. You may have settled on an acting style, but there are other methods to explore. You can even forget your comfortable techniques and rediscover authenticity.

You can speak as if your words were sacred, just like the words of humanity's greatest messengers. In your story, you really are the messenger; you are also the message. You create an environment for other people to inhabit. The way you communicate can change lives for the better, or destroy budding passions. It can expand possibilities or limit them. All of this is for you to decide.

The campus of this school is vast, and full of exciting options. Take it all in. Wander from the main walkways and distinguish yourself from other artists. With the wisdom that comes from experience, you will become more confident. With confidence, you'll be more willing to take chances and to speak for yourself. If inhibitions from childhood still plague you as an adult, you're not keeping up with your own evolution.

I encourage you to come up with original home-work assignments for this class. You are the best authority on you. You know your most predictable responses. You know your own pet words and phrases. You know your most touching stories. You also know your triggers and defenses. You know how to avoid judgment by judging yourself first. You know this character of yours better than anybody. So study yourself. Have fun, experiment a little, and challenge yourself.

Check on your inner dialogue now and then. How does it sound from one day to the next? What feelings does it generate? Maybe you can make it through a whole day—a week, a month—without listening to the voice in your head. When it gets no attention, the noise will stop. For any artist, it matters to get comfortable with silence, and be willing to let life rush in.

What Else Can I Do?

We can all benefit by doing research on our fellow artists. We can learn to watch other people without comment or judgment. We can observe their reactions to everyday events, and notice how we react in similar ways. We can feel their rhythm, hear their language. We can sense the message that lies hidden beneath their words.

Once you develop a talent for listening to others, you can hear yourself better. You can ask yourself,

"What is my tone and my style?" And then you can go farther. "What is my message?" you can ask. "What kind of artist am I, really?" Questions like those inspire new discoveries.

A rewarding relationship with life begins with trusting yourself. It comes from appreciating your instrument—the body, the brain—and allowing it to play an authentic song. Never mind the techniques taught to you long ago. Don't worry about remembering your lines. If you pay attention to the moment, the right words will fall into place at the right time.

We all get stuck. We can't seem to get over the spell of old stories, but that spell can be broken. Maybe you could start by writing about your life. Writing out your history is the best way to challenge outdated beliefs. Do it in whatever way you choose. Begin at the beginning—or the end, or the middle. Anyway you do it, you'll find some emotional resolution. You'll find perspective. You'll expose buried secrets and old grudges, along with things that have outlived their time and lost their purpose.

Don't assume your life hasn't been full of wonders. Don't underestimate the role you've played in your own destiny. Tell your story objectively, showing respect for every character. Most of all, respect the hero, the protagonist. The choices made by that character were neither good nor bad. The plot didn't work out the right way—or the worst way. There's nothing to judge and everything to forgive. An artist understands this, and handles every subject with compassion.

Another good exercise is to imagine yourself as a playwright, starring in your own play. You're the storyteller. You're also the lead actor, the headliner. You're the intriguing plot twist, or the character who redirects the action. You're everything shocking, amazing, and reassuring. It doesn't matter how the audience responds. Enthusiasm matters, and love for what you do. Play it for you—yes, be that daring.

Try to imagine one important event in your story. Then imagine this: your lines are improvised, not studied. Every motion and gesture is spontaneous. How would that alter the scene? How would simple honesty have affected the rest of the plot? Don't fear the past, learn from it. Dedicate yourself to making future scenes ring with truth.

You are a student of art. You are a painter, and the canvas is your life. You are a musician, and the symphony is you. You are a novelist, a composer, a sculptor.

How do you make a masterpiece? For one, you respect your art, whatever its peculiarities. Trust your vision. See the beauty in everything and paint it into your canvas. Love the art of you and speak in the simplest idioms of love.

Day 3:
Acting

"All that happens to us, including our humiliations, our misfortunes...all is given to us as raw material, as clay, so that we may shape our art."

—Jorge Luis Borges

Hi! Greetings to you, on another beautiful morning! The sky is clear and the mood is electric. The homework you gave yourself energized you to learn more, I can tell. We're all born to wonder, and to imagine. Mysteries are made to be solved. Today we dive a little deeper into the mystery of the actor. Are you ready?

We humans have the ability to bring visions to life and to compose the mood and the music of our days. This involves acting out key roles. We learn social behaviors, mimicry, and language skills early in our development, and all of these elements come together to make us the performers we are. This course is not intended to teach acting—you're a master already— but if you're interested in excelling at the art of life, it helps to recognize this:

You are acting all the time.

You believe the roles you play.

You believe the roles other people play.

That's simple enough. If you're thinking, "Hey, wait. I'm offended by that!" I'd say you're now playing the role of an offended person. If you're saying, "I agree that most people are faking it, but I'm not. I never pretend!" I'd say, sure, okay. You are authentic, but the character you assume (at work, at home, or even alone) is not.

Most of us love to watch comedians doing impressions of other people. So why does it hurt to be told we're imitating others? We all became a part of human society through imitation. It's how we learned to package and promote ourselves.

We are, in large part, a knockoff of the people who raised us. We take after many of the people who befriended us, or fell in love with us. Siblings don't resemble each other just because of their DNA, they resemble each other because they learned the same moves from the people who parented them. They learned the same speech patterns. They learned how to shape their mouths around syllables, and how to laugh, argue, persuade. They learned how to charm, or to annoy. They do it all in similar ways, because they went to the same art school.

The art of mimicry enables every living thing to grow safely to adulthood. It prepares all creatures to have infants of their own. Like baby whales, bunnies, or baboons, we humans learn to do everything our elders do in order to survive. It's instinctive, and it's no fault of ours if we continue to imitate throughout adulthood.

Still, imitation is something we should outgrow. Mature people act on their own, speak for themselves, and make decisions about their own life's journey. So should we all. When we remind people of everyone else, we cease to be interesting, we're barely interesting to ourselves. Instead, we could take advantage of our differences. We could retrieve the authenticity that was misplaced in childhood, no matter the situation.

It's an actor's instinct to meet truth in the moment. When honesty suddenly cuts through all the pretense, it can shock us. It can also shock an audience. To be willing conspirators in the moment, they, too, need that lightning bolt of truth. To come together as people, we all need to get real.

Early Training

When we were children, we made people happy. In simpler times, we could sing off key, dance badly, or paint the sky green, and we'd get a great response. We could fall off the sofa and get a big laugh. For a while, it seemed as if the world was the best possible audience, always easy to please. We learned to mimic the people closest to us, and they rewarded us with love. Seeing themselves in us, they were inspired to love themselves a little more.

Have you ever watched a child looking in the mirror? Children please themselves in the same way they've learned to please others. They pose. They try a hundred different facial expressions. They spin around like fashion models. They use all the elements of their emerging craft to create roles to play on the world stage.

Professional actors learn to sharpen the same skills they developed as amateurs: moving and speaking. So do you, in fact. As you mature, you continue to sharpen the skills life already gave you. An actor who moves across the stage confidently is more likely to captivate a crowd. An actor who's truly convincing gets everyone's attention. The same applies to you. How you move through the world determines the way people respond to you. Your tone, your choice of words, your body movements—they have the power to captivate an audience every time you step into a scene.

Every actor needs a place to shine, and your place was waiting for you long before you arrived on stage. The backdrop had already been hung, you could say, and props were already in place. Trusted characters were there already, standing on their marks and waiting for you under key lights. They were eager to act with you, to help you prepare and rehearse. Upon your arrival, the stage was set, your fellow actors were in place, and the play was already in progress. It was your turn to be part of the action.

It's not surprising that your worst nightmares sometimes involve being onstage, naked and without a script. You came into this world exactly that way: naked, dazzled by the lights, aware that everyone was watching. For a long time, you couldn't speak the lines they were feeding you. You couldn't perform like your older siblings. You've been pacing the stage ever since, often unsure of your skills and terrified of judgment. But like any seasoned actor, you continue to step up and give it your best shot.

You follow the same routine each day. In the morning, you put on your makeup (or whatever face you feel will serve you best), and dress for the part you are expected to play. Your choices aren't just about fitting in with the crowd. The big stage isn't just for those who conform—no, even nonconformists require masks and costumes. Defiance is a style choice. So are outrage and cynicism. When everyone is rebelling, even rebels seem conventional. Even insurgents are slaves to fashion.

In the end, our hairstyle, face, and clothing say very little about who we really are. Like bumper stickers and tattoos, they suggest how desperate we are *not to be seen.* We prefer to hide behind our slogans and our makeup. We camouflage the truth with sarcasm. Just for a moment, think back on your wonderful, spontaneous emergence into the world. You were an authentic being once. Where did that creature go?

Are you busy rehearsing, reciting, acting? Who compensates you for those efforts? You were born to mimic, that's true. You were blessed with a good brain, which makes it possible to process everything you see and respond to it. With practice and experience, you've become a master. When you do something enough times, it becomes part of your character. That's how professional actors prepare for a role. That's how you did it, too: with practice and repetition.

You established a character and a backstory. Now the dialogue comes automatically. Other characters in your play are lightly sketched, but you know *you*. No one can perform that role better, no matter the script, no matter the audience. But now you're beginning to see how this role has influenced your decisions and your actions. You see how much control it has over you. You may even realize that you don't need to work so hard at it. You could even take some time to discover the artist behind the role.

Let each piece of the puzzle lead you to the next piece. Keep learning more about the mystery of you the actor. By becoming aware of your methods, you can make informed decisions about where to go from here.

The Method

Awareness helps you to recognize your choices. Right now, you're becoming aware of yourself as an actor. You're seeing yourself from a new perspective, which will help you make better choices as you grow. So let's take a look at different techniques actors use to excel at their craft.

You already see similarities to the way most of us approach ordinary situations. For instance, it's a common technique for us to act like we care about other people's problems when we don't. We show emotion—getting angry, sad, or offended—because it seems appropriate.

There are plenty of times when our feelings don't match our actions. There are times when our actions don't match our thoughts. In some drama schools, that's called "surface acting." Surface acting is what the rest of us call being superficial, or insincere. When there's a contradiction between what an actor feels and what he does, the result is a bad performance. The long-term result is physical exhaustion. Being authentic is energizing, but faking it is hard work.

Doing a mediocre job can make an actor anxious, self-conscious, even ashamed. The performance suffers, of course. If an actor can't create a bond with other players, the whole play will suffer. How does this relate to you? When you're not in tune with yourself, your art suffers. When you're not in tune with your fellow players, your life suffers. This should make sense to you, it should even sound familiar.

You've probably heard of Method Acting, but what does it mean? The Method encourages an actor to use personal memories to inspire a performance. This makes sense, since artists rely heavily on their own life experience. You, too, rely on what you know and what you've experienced. You refer to past history in your social interactions, don't you? You talk about your childhood, your past love affairs, your current job. When your stories aren't enough, you repeat other people's stories, you borrow from someone else's life. Either way, you do your best to engage people. You hook their attention and you entertain them. That's your method.

Method Acting advises an actor to bring a specific memory to life as the scene is in progress. For instance, the emotions that an actor felt when a loved one died years ago are reactivated and substituted for those of the character while the scene is playing out. The actor was heartbroken then, and his character is heartbroken now. Using emotional memories makes a performer more believable in a make-believe situation. Whether you're performing on stage or off, that method may seem normal to you.

We draw on painful memories often, obsessing over past offenses. Maybe we get angry now because we couldn't then. We prolong our grieving, thinking we're honoring a loved one, or punishing ourselves. We relive past confrontations and old jealousies just for fun. And that's only what we do by ourselves. In public, we turn those private feelings into performance art.

We've all been in situations where we're expected to feel strong emotions and to demonstrate those emotions publicly. A funeral is that kind of situation. A wedding is another. We're expected to cry openly, in our grief and in our joy. We yell like maniacs at a sports game. We roar with laughter at a comedy show. We're as zealous as our co-workers, or as cynical as a friend. We're as offended, or as deeply hurt, as someone close to us. "If you loved me," your partner might say, "you'd feel what I feel!" It seems you should, but you don't. You can't.

You can empathize, of course. You can sense what someone is going through and comfort them. In real life, reaching another person's level of outrage doesn't help, it makes things worse. For most of us, pretending to feel something isn't fun. In the short term, it puts us at war with ourselves. In the long run, it makes us really tired. It can also make us sick.

For professional actors, showing intense emotion in every performance is hard on the body. In most situations, it's hard on yours. Bringing painful memories to mind, whatever your excuse, feels like a punishment. To your nervous system, it really *is* a punishment.

Your acting may seem real, but it follows a thought process that you control. You brought a memory to life, you made a random idea seem true. You're the playwright, the director. You determine the mood and the method of every performance, and you pay the emotional price for it. It makes no artistic sense to inflict pain on yourself. It's folly to relive a childhood trauma to appear more authentic. It may seem obvious to say, but authenticity doesn't need a gimmick. Truth needs no effort.

Resolving emotional problems is part of every actor's job, it's also your job. We all want to be more productive artists and better partners. This means clearing our emotional stumbling blocks so we're ready to take on bigger roles. Try to be a conscientious editor of your own material. If you've been indulging old wounds and bad memories, you're making your life too difficult. And you're getting in the way of your art.

There is another acting technique that simply requires actors to be present. In other words, they immerse themselves in the scene's circumstance rather than recalling past experiences. *They believe what's happening on stage.*

And it works. The key is to look, to listen, and to understand what's going on right in front of you. Take note of this. Present circumstances should determine your actions, not past impressions. The point is to show up and be attentive to the moment. The point is to *be there*.

Being there doesn't mean trying to remember a feeling. It doesn't mean searching for an appropriate story. Quoting wiser people isn't the same as expressing your real feelings. Words are more likely to reach the heart of the listener when they're spoken with sincerity. We all know when someone isn't being emotionally honest on stage, it makes us uneasy. We want to look away. The same is true in ordinary life: When people try too hard, we get uncomfortable. When someone's faking it, we'd prefer to look away.

Acting is believing: this is a maxim in most drama schools. Of course, believing something doesn't make it true. In your daily life it pays to be skeptical. You don't have to believe everything you hear, whether the ideas come from you or anyone else. You can see more, and hear better, when you're able to perceive what's actually happening and not turn it into a melodrama.

Accept more challenges like these. Challenge yourself to be skeptical, but willing to listen. After all, you're not performing for a paying public. You're not trying to put on a show. You know now that authenticity will serve you for a lifetime. It will also serve your company of players. Anyone sharing your journey will appreciate your ability to be there and be real—right now, one hundred percent.

Attention to the Craft

Maybe you think acting is for people more extroverted than you, or who like being the center of attention. You might think it's for someone more attractive and confident. Deep within you, you know better. You've always sensed that you're an actor. You may not recall your first teachers, or directors. You might deny that a script was ever being written for you, but you're still not sure why you say many of the things you say. Certain impulses baffle you, and many of your reactions surprised you. You can't make sense of this little soap opera that is your life, even now.

Your journey is a confounding mystery, mostly because you haven't noticed what's going on behind the scenes. Attention is the key to learning. Students get nowhere if they lose attention in class. Attention helped you to be a good actor, it helped you stay loyal to your role. By redirecting your attention, you can do something you've never tried before: discard old roles and realities.

Until now, you've allowed your beliefs to control your attention. When you believe something, in other words, you tend to focus your attention on everything that might support that belief. You find ways to confirm the merit of your belief. In fact, it's difficult to pull your attention away long enough to consider a different point of view.

When you have control of your attention, you're not so easily ruled by any belief or opinion. You don't feel obliged to react to what other people think. You can consciously decide where to invest your faith. Where you put your attention, things happen. Relationships blossom. Gardens grow. Projects flourish. Most importantly, *beliefs* are born through the force of your attention. And without it, they lose their power over you.

You've used your attention to support a certain way of being, but maybe you'd like things to be different now. Maybe you want to be more receptive, more spontaneous. The world will try to distract you from that effort. It's noisy place where everyone is fighting for attention. People around you are caught up in their own show. Your character is a bit player in their production.

Your story isn't important. None of that should matter, what matters is how you distract and deny yourself.

Picture yourself at the movies on a Saturday night: The theater is full and the audience is restless and loud. With all that chaos around you, it's hard to concentrate on the film. Crowds like to talk. They text. They squirm, move around, and make trips to the concession stand. Meanwhile, up there on the screen, the action keeps rolling. The movie goes on, with or without anyone's attention.

I could be describing the world you know—the world outside the theater. Every day, life's astonishing art is being created in front of your eyes. It buds, it blossoms, it flashes and dies, while your attention is on the noise. Even without all the outside drama, your attention is being hijacked by the scenes going on in your head. This is true for everyone, nobody is paying much attention to anybody.

Attention pays amazing dividends. Teaching that lesson to your kids is as important as applying it to yourself. Whether or not they choose to be happy adults, they will have an available connection to joy, to love, and to life, through you. They will learn the rewards of paying attention from you.

Truth in Acting

Attention makes the difference between an ordinary actor and a captivating one. It makes the difference between a solid friend and someone who can't be trusted. Never mind what the rest of the world is doing, we all need to put more attention on being honest. We say we'll do things, and then we forget what we said. We make promises we can't keep. We lie to ourselves regularly by acting and overreacting. There's a simple improvisation that explains this point. Try to relax and imagine for a moment...

Imagine that you are standing on a hillside, looking down at a lovely country landscape below. The sight is a pleasant one, and very calming. Looking closer, you notice that there is a long stretch of train track running through this little valley. Can you see it? Good. Let's continue.

As you stand there, looking at the view, you hear the sound of an approaching train. The sound seems to be coming from two different directions. This catches your attention. Now you can see two trains, one is coming from the east and one is coming from the west. Both trains are racing along the same track. Their whistles blow. Neither train is slowing down.

Suddenly it occurs to you: at the speed they're going, the two trains can't avoid crashing into each other.

Okay, now. Stand exactly where you are, and act out your response. You're watching. The trains are rushing toward each other. Their horns are blowing. The screech of metallic brakes fills the valley, but you know the trains can't possibly slow down in time to avoid a tragic collision.

Are you imagining yourself crying, or turning away? Are you stumbling down the hill, arms waving? Are you yelling at the trains? Are you shouting for help? Maybe you cover your face, refusing to be a witness to this event. When the trains finally crash into each other and fly off the track, what do you do? Do you scream in horror? Do you fall to the ground? Do you faint?

If you were acting in front of an audience, you would get intensely emotional playing this scene, wouldn't you? Of course! Watching a disaster take place is emotionally shattering. And you would show that. You would show terror and rage. You would lose your voice shrieking. You would lose your mind.

Actually, a good director would give you a failing grade if you did any of that. An acting coach would watch your frantic performance, give you a minute to catch your breath, and then say, "Okay. Now show me what you'd *really* do in that situation."

What? After all that emotional effort? You'd probably be insulted by the comment, but you're a good student. You'd try again. This time you'd pay more attention. You'd stare into the imagined distance and watch the two trains approaching, getting nearer and nearer to each other. You'd see they were going too fast and getting too close to avoid a disaster. What could you do? You could do nothing.

Alone, and so far away, you couldn't help. So you would do nothing. Your expression would probably go from concern, to amazement, to paralysis. Even before the moment of the collision, your body would freeze. Your mouth might open, but you'd make no sound. You'd watch in silence. You'd barely breathe. When it was all over, you might make a choice to run to the scene or run for help.

This response is far less theatrical than all the screaming, but it's more honest. Honesty, as we've said, can be riveting. Truth is compelling, and because we see it so seldom, it has the power to shock us. Maybe this exercise shocks you. Doing nothing may go against your instincts, but your instincts are lost in the thought process. It's easy to *think* you'd do all sorts of things— things that don't make sense when the time comes. But thinking rarely plays the lead role in an emergency.

It's good to check your level of honesty in any situation. When you're stunned by your own falseness, something changes in you. When you witness your own hypocrisy, you start yearning for truth. Truth is elusive in our daily lives, mostly because we forget to look for it. That can change. We can develop an appetite for it. We can demand it from ourselves. We can stop pretending for a moment, and wait for it.

Great actors love to act, and I can see why. They're more attracted to the truth than to a lie—and, ironically, they find it on stage. How can acting and authenticity be compatible? Well, the answer is both complicated and simple. We've all been searching for truth since the early days of this adventure. As kids, we learned that deception was often expected, sometimes preferred. Since then, we've been missing the taste and feel of truth. To put it simply, we've been missing *us* for too long.

The problem is, most audiences love the drama. They insist on a good show. So what's an actor to do?

Audiences change everything. We respond differently when we're being observed. For example, imagine the scene with the two trains again. This time, imagine you're not alone on a country hillside. Someone is with you when the trains collide.

With someone beside you, your reactions would be bigger, maybe you'd actually scream, point, and describe what's coming. You'd probably check the other person for a response. It's no mystery that people feed off each other's emotions. We take cues from each other. We were trained to deliver a performance, and too often, we feel obligated to do so.

Why? Well, drama paid off in our infancy, didn't it? When we couldn't ask for something, we screamed. Screaming got someone's attention, at the very least. When we were finally able to use words, we screamed anyway. A tantrum got us a quick response. Screaming and kicking got immediate results. We discovered a way to control other people, bigger people, and the lesson stuck.

Childhood tantrums grow into teenage tantrums, eventually, they evolve into destructive behaviors in adults. It's weird to see grown-ups kick and scream to get attention, isn't it? Kicking and screaming are metaphors, of course, for all kinds of theatrical behavior. The actions of a toddler doesn't improve adult relationships. We all know this by now. When every action gets a reaction—followed by the need to react to that reaction—the insanity escalates.

Maybe you, too, act like a crazy person under pressure. Maybe you're the drama queen, throwing tantrums to get attention. No? Okay, I'm not talking about you specifically, but some people continue to play those roles. It doesn't matter that they get a negative response—only that they get a response. Most people evolve and mature. They learn from experience and adapt. They dare to be honest. Sometimes, they grow wise.

I'm asking you now: Are you as honest with yourself as you know how to be—or does it satisfy you just to give a realistic performance? All roads lead to truth, if you want to find it. It may require a winding, confusing journey, but what else are you here to do? Don't waste time waiting for better roles, better plays, or a more congenial troupe of players. Listen to yourself now. Learn from your lies. Change course, and let honesty slip into your conversations. Encourage a taste for it.

To be free to create, you have to laugh away the critics. You have to lose your fear of judgment. You may have to leave the beaten track to find truth hidden in the thorn bushes. Who cares? Go ahead. Indulge in a daily dose of truth, if only for you.

The Company

The troupe, or the theatrical family, is the beating heart of professional acting, and the trust that exists among that family is an example for all of us. Actors must count on each other. They must count on their backstage support as well. The magic of theater is about collaboration, for every artist is essential to the final result.

Actors, at their best, work as a close team. They trust each other for the right cues and the right timing. They rely on each other's energy and inspiration. Professional acting can involve long hours and physical stress, but good collaboration makes it worthwhile.

So it is with the rest of us. We all travel with a small cast of friends. Sharing experiences brings us closer. Trusting each other makes us less cynical about life. Allowing a friend to shine is a generous gift. None of this sounds particularly theatrical, but it leads to the same: a magical outcome. The magic we create between us is its own precious mystery.

Artists of any kind are drawn to one another. They enjoy sharing the language and passions of their art. They talk about the work, its problems and rewards. Do you discuss your own process, or tricks of your trade, with anyone? In what company can you openly talk about your fears, or your victories over fear? In what circumstance would you dare to be emotionally vulnerable, and feel comfortable about it?

Supported by their troupe, actors can make brave choices. They can be fools in league with other fools for the sake of their art. When did you trust life enough to cast aside your inhibitions? It's inspiring to see people working together as a confident team, or to witness trust and fellowship between people in pursuit of a common purpose. It's discouraging to be at odds with each other.

It only takes a slight shift of perception to appreciate every person's talent. If more of us made that shift, we'd be excited to share similar passions. We'd remove our masks now and then. We'd dare to be genuine. Instead, we choose to remain guarded. We keep secrets, even from ourselves.

Admitting that we're a company of players—participating in big and small productions together—can break down a lot of imaginary walls. It can even break down some real ones, so that we're willing to invent games and conspire together. Fun can be our main objective. We don't need to be children again to know the thrill of playing as a team. We can get caught up in the excitement and feel that magic anytime.

Children's theater is an example of surrendering to the magic. An audience of children does more than observe, they insist on being part of the action. You can imagine it, I'm sure. Do it now: Picture yourself sitting in the audience at a play produced for children. The curtain comes up on a fairy tale—*Rapunzel and the Witch*, let's say.

Notice how quickly the children accept the premise of a girl being captured by a witch and forced to live out her days in an enchanted tower. They get it immediately, even if they've never heard the story before. Their excitement doesn't depend on elaborate sets or special effects. They don't have to know a backstory. They don't have to see waves of golden hair tumbling from the tower window, they imagine it.

They understand that a prince has fallen in love with Rapunzel and wants to release her from the witch's cruelty. When the wicked witch creeps on stage, they're filled with terror and excitement. They call out to the other characters on stage, warning them of the danger. They're part of the scene. They're caught up in the action.

Children arrive at a theater as themselves and then become something else. They become co-conspirators. They willingly, eagerly, surrender to the spell—throwing themselves into the plot. While the play lasts, Rapunzel's happiness affects their happiness. Her destiny is their destiny. You may think that sounds childish, but are adults really any different?

Don't you routinely push yourself into absurd plot twists? Aren't you often lured into someone else's drama? It's hard to resist getting hooked. You believe the premise of their story, whatever it is, and sign on to the madness. It happens.

Kids use their amazing imaginations for fun. For them, it's great to be in an imagined world and to believe in it completely. In the company of other excited kids, they can take a thrilling ride. But staying too long in a fantasy is exhausting, even for a child. After an afternoon of pretending, children are relieved to be called home for supper and to collapse into a warm bed. We adults, too, need to be called home to ourselves. Young or old, no one wants to be locked in a tower forever, however magical it might have seemed at first.

I'm asking you to notice where you put your faith, and make changes when you need to. Common sense says to put your faith in *you*. Don't lie to yourself for the sake of an idyllic notion. It's not enough to admit to the fantasy, you need to wake yourself up. See where a bad story is taking you, and alter your course. Say no to the drama. Win the war over fear. Protect yourself from your own abuses, no one can do it for you.

Stage Fright

I'm sure you've felt the struggle between wanting to fit in and daring to be real. You've been reluctant to take a different path. You've been afraid to make the unwelcome comment. You've known the anxiety of having to face the public and expose yourself to criticism.

Sometimes the situation isn't so public. For example, you've been apprehensive about a first date, or a job interview. You've made yourself sick over a homework assignment, or an upcoming business trip. You've been afraid to confront a friend, or to break up with a partner. A fear of judgment can end your most creative impulses. It can cause you to go against yourself.

Maybe you've also experienced the terror of being on an actual stage, in front of a live audience. In that case, your critics were hundreds of strangers. You had all the right tools—your face, your voice, your message—but under that kind of scrutiny, your tools seemed inadequate. Maybe the dream of being naked and laughed at became real for you. If so, your work would have been spoiled by fear. It happens to every artist.

Your life is your art, and the masterpiece you create must someday be revealed to the world. Painters must exhibit their works, even if it means exposing themselves to rejection. Actors must walk onto the stage. Musicians must open their hearts to a fickle public. Comedians have to face the hecklers. And what do any of those challenges have to do with you? Just about everything.

You're on display often, if not most of the time. You exhibit your art to co-workers and family members on a regular basis. Your talents are under scrutiny every day. You practice and rehearse for every upcoming show and get the jitters anyway. In solitary moments, you imagine the worst possible outcome.

So it may be time to take another view of life. Your existence is an ongoing dream, and the dream changes as your perceptions change. Other people are performing on their little stages, trying to please their own public. Watch them in action. See how fear represses their best instincts. See how their criticism of you reflects their own insecurities. Don't worry that people will reject you. It's far more important to notice how you reject yourself.

Professional actors deserve enormous credit for facing their fears. They step onto the stage, night after night, putting their reputations on the line. Well, an amateur like you does the same. You take similar chances every day. You face possible failure, as every artist does. You risk being ridiculed. You put yourself on display and brace yourself for the consequences. In your career, you've died a little and come back again many times. In the process, you've improved your craft.

Take a moment to recognize the dreamlike quality of your life. Imagine yourself on stage, under the lights. Who's watching? Is anyone even paying attention? Your fears seem overwhelming, but you confront them and get beyond them. Fear is often a creative choice, an accessory. Choose courage instead. Choose humor.

Choose faith in yourself. Create on your own terms. You have a chance to be a master before you leave this campus. That, too, is your choice.

Everyone you know has had to overcome fear, you can guide the ones you love by example. Be aware of the troupe—your team of supporters. Mutual trust is something we all wish for. Enjoy your cast of characters. Let them know you. Get to know them, and support them in their play.

See people as the artists they are. See how they commit themselves to their roles. Notice their character's motivations, as well as their strengths and their shortcomings. Appreciate them as they are. Encourage their art, whatever it is. Your attention matters, so show them the best reflections of themselves. Be there for the people in your life, and trust them to do the same for you.

Love as Motivation

In simple terms, motivation is what gets an actor from one side of the stage to the other. What compels us ordinary people to do what we do? That's hard to say, since our behavior is so often automatic. We don't give a lot of thought to our actions or reactions. We move erratically across the stage and fill uncomfortable silences with noise.

Professional actors, however, plan their movements precisely. You and I don't ask questions like, "Why did I sit down, or why did I get up again?" We don't wonder why we turned upstage or moved suddenly to the left. We don't notice every tilt of the head or lift of the brow. Actors use the smallest gestures to tell the audience something. They use their body, their instrument, consciously. The rest of us? Well, we aren't so conscious, but that doesn't mean we're not motivated.

In your daily routine, one scene leads to another and conversations repeat themselves (much like they do in a television soap opera). You're not sure *why* you say the things you say. You can't always explain what makes you do what you do. Something compels you. Something makes you play different roles, in different situations, for different people. You choose your mood according to an unspoken need.

You act like a baby with one person, crying for what you want. With another person, you're smooth and seductive. With someone else, you're short-tempered and competitive. You're the good child, or the bad child. You're the martyr, the mediator, or the dummy. Those are all acting choices. They're usually motivated by something—perhaps by a need to be validated, or praised, or just to be noticed. Whatever it is, the end result is that you get what you want.

You make deliberate choices when you play a role. You act for specific reasons, whether or not you admit to them. Have you asked yourself lately about those reasons? What brought you here, for instance? Why are you attending this class? How would you like your world to change, and how committed are you to making those changes happen? How willing are you to end the drama in your life?

An astute actor doesn't search for motivation just to get across the stage, but to get at the heart of a scene. She finds the core of a character using empathy, not judgment. It's your job, too, to understand the motivation behind your actions and words without judgement. Once that is understood, you can adjust your actions to suit who you are now, not the role you used to play. You can act now, into the moment, and save yourself the pain of any future regrets. You can allow love to guide your next decision, and the next.

Love is every artist's most compelling motivation. Take a good look at your character's attitudes about love. It may be time to update some old beliefs on the subject, you might even decide to abandon those beliefs. Does love feel dangerous to you? Has it always seemed scary? Do you worry about losing control? Do you think loving someone makes you seem weak, or foolish? If so, give up on that idea. Being afraid of love makes no sense at all.

Love is simple, but we often make it complicated. Our relationship with love is one of confusion and resistance. It's a lot like our relationship with ourselves, we're reluctant to get too close or feel too deeply. We've been taught to think love is just an emotion—maybe even a debilitating one.

Like any good actor, you may like to turn love into high drama. You may turn it into a joke. If you only pretend to love, love yields quickly to hate. Your acting might deceive the world, but the world doesn't matter. You matter, and how you love determines your happiness.

The problem is, few of us were taught how to love. Our relationship with love is loaded with contradictions. We don't really trust it. We write songs about it, glorify it, and then blame love for all our problems. We say love is fickle. We say love is blind, but we yearn for it anyway.

We pledge our love eternally, unless something happens to change our minds. Love conquers all, depending on the situation. Love is all we need... maybe. It's safe to say that most of us learned to love with doubts and conditions.

You may have heard yourself say you can't love, or that you don't deserve love, but those are stories. They were intended to protect you from pain, but you don't need them now. You might think love is to blame for your unhappiness, but you're lying to yourself. *What you believe* is making you unhappy.

Just for a moment, forget what you believe about love. Think of love as the combined force of all emotions. Think of love as energy itself, powerful and creative. You are that power, existing within matter. Love is as much a part of you as the atoms of your body.

It's rare for anyone to experience the uncompromising authority of love, and there's a reason for that. As you walk through your life, you only meet love's reflections. A reflection is not the thing itself. You've spent your life getting distorted reflections of love, and you've mirrored love back in the same way. You choose how intensely you're willing to love, according to the risks.

In fact, love is not a choice. Your mind can deny it, but it has no chance against love. For an artist, love is the primary incentive. When you create, you lose track of who you are. You surrender to life. When you're in the process of making something—an object, a plan, or a memory—love is always in charge.

You already know what it feels like to surrender. You abandon your fears when you make love, for example—you forget all the roles you've ever played. When you create, you also forget who you're supposed to be. You're guided by mystery when you work your hands to shape beautiful things out of the raw materials of life. You feel like energy itself when you sing, or dance. Energy is the force of love.

Love won't hurt you. Pushing love away will hurt you. Believing you're a victim of love will hurt you. Like every artist, you've probably lacked inspiration on occasion. You've felt starved for attention and praise. Yes, there have been times when you've felt betrayed by love, by life. You can leave those stories in the past. Now you know the truth: You are your own best source of love.

In the course of your journey, you've convinced yourself to believe in lies. You've made poor choices as well as brilliant ones. This is how you've evolved. See that, and celebrate your exceptional life. When it comes to artistic flair, no one excels like you. No one channels life the way you do. No one loves as fearlessly as you do now.

Who cares what the critics say? Surrender to your best artistic instincts. Challenge yourself with making a masterpiece, and infuse it with love every day.

Why Does All this Matter?

Like all of us, you're here to enjoy life. The problem is, you get swept up in the drama. Who can blame you? The trials and tribulations of humanity demand your full attention. It's especially hard to resist the melodrama taking place in your mind with its unruly cast and illogical storylines.

Your mind broadcasts a soap opera of its own. It puts on a good show—too good, you could say. It produces a drama that feeds your fears and your doubts. And that drama has a tendency to spread to the real world, which affects everyone you love. Their reactions may be just as dramatic, causing even more fear and doubt. And so the show goes on.

We all want to command attention, but some people get attention through disruption and chaos. If you feel you're one of those, consider writing a different script for yourself. Consider having more respect for your play and for the players taking part in it. So much self-indulgence causes unnecessary pain. In the long run, you'll feel the pain more than anyone.

Be aware of your own dramatic excesses. You're not the victim of your art. Neither are you the beleaguered audience feeling used, cheated, and demanding your money back. You are the actor, choreographer, and set designer in this production of yours. You also direct, produce, and control the quality of your material. Your tantrums don't help the creative process. Self-pity doesn't reflect your genius.

Artistic excellence sounds impossible to achieve at first, but remember that you've been working on your masterpiece for decades. You've been learning new methods all your life. You've been practicing and experimenting. Your special talents show in the things you love to do. Art is a celebration of life. Artistic excellence is an ongoing odyssey. Don't stop now.

We stop growing as artists when we stop exploring. We don't learn by following the same trails and observing the same scenery. We build our own masterpiece by cutting a different path. "A masterpiece? Are you kidding?" you might be saying. "Who can be bothered? And why should it matter?"

Why? Well, you're much happier doing something you're good at. You're happier being productive. When you're not battling outside pressures, you can begin to love yourself, and that matters. Your art matters. Your authentic presence matters to the lives of the people around you.

While you're preparing for your next role, or planning your next publicity tour, consider the energy you spend rehearsing for life instead of living it. Consider the amount of time you spend dreaming of love instead of putting the power of love into action. Love is your most enduring legacy. It's been discouraged and postponed, so the challenge now is to bring it back.

Where Do I Start?

Remember that we are all acting, and we don't know it. We play different roles for different people, in different situations. You and I are not professional actors, but we've been taught to please and to follow direction. From a very young age we were told to act this way or that way according to every situation. Nothing about that is right or wrong, it's just a fact. Kids need to fit in for their own safety. They need to blend into society and adapt to cultural peculiarities. And the habit of blending in stays with us into adulthood.

What does authenticity look like in action? For one, we stop struggling to imagine how people are judging us. We're not afraid to offer our own unique take on things. Our reactions are born of our perceptions, not our stories. We are present, aware, and responsive to the moment.

Honesty and spontaneity used to be natural to all of us. It used to be natural to you. You were completely authentic as a child, but what was once instinctive may now take some practice. You may have forgotten how to respond spontaneously, and it will take practice to assure yourself that you won't die from *not acting a part*.

"Not acting" doesn't mean acting like you're not acting. Like any good professional, you can be aware that you're performing even while you savor precious moments of truth. You can distinguish the times you need to be what people expect you to be from the times you only need to *be*.

You can respect other people's roles while choosing to be genuine. You are not like anyone else. Your brain doesn't function like any one's and your body doesn't look like anyone's. Your memories are different and your interpretations of memories are filtered through your own beliefs. In this lifetime you will play the role of someone's mother or father or attentive friend. You will play the wife, the husband, the lover. These are predictable roles, but you will play them your way.

Professional actors find a way to be authentic in predictable roles. When they replace someone in a role, they won't play the character exactly as it was played before. They're unlikely to copy another performance, however well it was received by the public. They must give the role as much of themselves as they can.

For instance, Romeo and Juliet are central characters in Shakespeare's famous tragedy. Every young actor who plays Romeo will do it his way. Every actress playing Juliet will portray the role as she imagines it. Every interpretation is valuable. Every characterization is unique because actors perceive and behave differently.

Is that true for the rest of us? Are we bringing our unique style and vision to our actions, or are we echoing a performance we've seen and admired? Are we imitating the responses of people close to us? Are we using the same phrases and making similar gestures? These aren't questions we usually ask ourselves.

Only you know if you're being true to your own instincts. Only you can decide to walk through the world in unaffected ways. It's important to remind yourself that you have a choice. In every situation, you can choose to pick up a familiar role or put it aside. At any moment you can choose to hide behind a mask, or to set it down and abandon the act.

Either way, the rest of the world may still look at what you're doing and see a performance, but without a mask, you'll feel liberated. Without a role to play, you will know yourself better. You can respect the truth of you—its manifestations and its mysteries. You have the choice to use your talents consciously. When a performance isn't needed, you can also choose to set aside your pretenses and stop the show.

You've been under the spell of your own character for a long time. The stories you tell about yourself are not the truth. They are your exceptional art, and you invest a lot in your art. You invest a lot in your stories to the point that they seem true. In fact, your body bends to your stories. Your moods, your attitude, your prejudices are supported by stories that were handed down to you by other people.

Stories can change, however. You can alter the script and cancel the next performance. You can take it all in—the people, the conversations, the drama—and enjoy it for what it is. You can allow actions to take the place of your stories. Good actors get caught up in the *doing* of things, even when they have to recite a lot of dialogue. The circumstances in a play or film may be fixed, but an actor must summon the will to respond to those circumstances. So must you.

We all want our moments to count. We also want to benefit from someone's full attention, if only briefly. We want to be better at paying attention, too, and to focus on one thing at a time. Most of all, we want action, not theory, and action requires that we use our will.

I'm reminding you that your will is an awesome force. It's your superpower. Yes, you have the responsibility to use it wisely, but you might have forgotten to use it at all. Just as some actors allow themselves to be upstaged, we often let someone with a stronger will control us. We get lazy about our actions. We let other people make artistic choices for us and even take charge of our own production. We surrender our will.

I leave you with this homework assignment: exercise your will. Feel its force, and direct it. Turn energy into something tangible. Turn "nothing" into something wonderful. Your will is your power. Command it with joy.

Day 4:
The
Stage

"All the world's a stage, and all the men and women merely players. They have their exits and their entrances, and one man in his time plays many parts..."

–Shakespeare

How reassuring to see you again, ready to tackle more mysteries! Notice that you used your will to get here this morning. You're *willing* to learn more, to see more, and to put your curiosity to good use. Let's see where your will, and mine, take us now.

In his excellent way, Shakespeare stated what most people already know to be true: We play the roles people expect us to play. As he described it, we start as infants and then grow into reluctant students. In time, we become sighing lovers, soldiers, and respectable members of society. Eventually we grow old. We end our lives as weak as babies again, helpless and mystified. "This strange eventful history" is one we all share, bringing our own style to each role and walking onto whatever stage we choose. Which moves us to the next topic: the stage.

The stage is every actor's natural environment. Today, you're going to imagine it bigger than the space that an actor can cover in a few strides. For you, and for the rest of humanity, the stage includes the length and breadth of the Earth. Your performance refers to the artistic choices you've made since you arrived.

This planet is the stage you stepped onto decades ago. The events of your life may seem vague now, but today you'll have a chance to remember. You'll see how your past led you to this moment. By remembering where you've been, you can plot all future road trips consciously.

Map-making changed human destiny, this exercise can change yours. Imagine your travels through life— your history of choices and decisions—as a roadmap. See it as a charted route whose starting point is your physical birth. It's a long and meandering road from there, but easily imagined once you start.

You've probably had breakfast at a roadside diner where you're given a menu, a set of silverware, and a place mat with children's games and puzzles printed on it. One of the puzzles is a simple maze. To solve it, you trace a line from the entrance of the maze to an exit point on the far side. Even little puzzles like that can be challenging. Some paths end quickly. Some wind back to the beginning. Some connect to other paths, going nowhere. Only one path will lead out of the maze.

Your life's journey is far more elaborate than a child's puzzle, but it involves similar twists and turns. So go ahead: Imagine your life sketched out on a piece of paper. Imagine it as a maze. Notice the dead-ends and switchbacks—the results of your less successful choices. Recall the stretches when everything seemed to go smoothly. Make the puzzle as tricky as the trajectory of your life has been, but remember this: it has only one entrance and one exit.

The Maze

This maze of yours took shape when you emerged from your mother's womb. Back then, decisions were made for you until you were old enough to make them for yourself. You kept moving forward. There were paths you wished you'd never taken and paths you took without hesitation or regret. You moved forward anyway.

You followed someone else's road map, or you stumbled through a series of random turns on your own. Either way, you kept moving. Like a tourist enjoying vacation photos, you can now see where you went during your stay here, and how much fun you had.

If you stretch the path into a straight line, the route you've taken is even easier to track. Try doing that: Imagine the maze as a highway that extends across an entire map. Again, follow your life's path. Do this tonight: draw a straight line across a large sheet of paper. The start of the line marks your birth, the end marks this present moment.

Draw little x's to indicate the major events in your life, and label them. Mark the less significant events as well. They might have been pivotal moments— moments that changed your cast of characters, or shifted your motivation. Those "lesser" moments may even have saved you, and extended your time in the maze.

See where every choice has led you. Those choices are clear to you now, even if they weren't back then. Notice the various crossroads you could have taken but didn't. See where you could have changed course, or turned back. Recall the passions that pushed you to move faster, or to slow down. Recall the people who persuaded you to stay in place. Mark the times where you got distracted and lingered too long. No decision was a wrong one, they all provide some good information—information you wished you'd had years ago.

Now you can go back to drawing your life as a maze. Give it the same detail. Give it the attention it deserves. You can even create a narrative to go with it. You're used to telling your story in bits and pieces, this exercise gives you a chance to talk through it from beginning to end. It gives you a way to smooth the emotional rough spots and resolve unhealed wounds.

Every incident is part of the intricate puzzle, or tapestry, that makes your life such a unique achievement. Work through the places that once tested you emotionally. Make peace with old injuries. Forgive the people who hurt you. Forgive yourself as well. I urge you to do this, and then to study your handiwork.

What did you find out? How has this process changed your perspective? It's odd to take a class in your own history, I know. It's not easy to examine your life objectively. You already know the subject well, but you probably haven't approached your life from the viewpoint of a master artist. Do it now. Step back and admire your efforts. Like a painter putting down his brush, allow yourself to be amazed.

A Life on Film

Now, if you don't mind, I'll change the metaphor slightly. Imagine this line on a sheet of paper as a strip of celluloid, with images of the key events of your life. It plays like a movie. There's a dramatic beginning to the film, as you opened your lungs and gasped for air. That simple act catapulted you into the dream of humanity, where your talents would determine your ability to survive and to flourish. What a thriller!

See the movie from beginning to end. Take a closer look at some of the key scenes. You can make cuts in the film, or slow down the rush of images. You can focus on a memory that seems unimportant, or one that changed the direction of events. There's nothing to fear in watching. It's only an exercise.

Looking closely at your life shouldn't make you feel regret. It's your saga, yes, but it's fun-filled and loaded with action sequences, just like any movie. It's a slapstick comedy, a tragedy, a cautionary tale. Enjoy all of it. Don't let unpleasant memories bother you. Wonderful moments, gone forever, shouldn't sadden you. You're only studying a puzzle on a placemat. You're imagining a movie, and contemplating a course for the future.

You can also view this movie as if you were watching another person's life documented on film—another life, with another actor. Appreciate the changing moods. Get comfortable with the madness as well as the monotony. Mistakes were made and promises were broken, heartbreaks came and went. Try to understand each sequence from your present perspective. Above all, be sympathetic to the main character.

Do you wonder how other people might view the movie of your life—people you've known and loved? They'd probably see the central character differently. And they would want to see themselves in it, of course. They'd expect to be featured prominently. If you walked into an adjacent theater, where a film was playing about the life of someone you know, you'd do the same.

"Where do I fit into this narrative?" you'd wonder. "How necessary am I to the plot? How valuable am I to the hero?" You're not the main character in anyone's movie but your own, but you want to be represented well in their stories. You want them to confirm your importance. You'd prefer to be missed when you walk out of a scene.

We're a traveling troupe of actors and artists who move around a very big stage. We shuffle aimlessly or we march with solemn determination, but we're all moving steadily away from the lights and out of the frame. We all know there's an exit to the maze, but we don't know when we'll stumble on it. And we will all leave a legacy, of course. Our legacy will be the collection of memory-images we leave behind.

What will yours look like? Will you leave memories that inspire and comfort? How generously did you love? How bravely did you open yourself to love? You're still taking this journey, and you're meeting more artists along the way who will carry an impression of you throughout their lives. However old or young you are, this legacy is yours to determine, and it will exist until everyone who knew you is gone.

During your time on stage, some of your fellow artists have demonstrated their love and support. You've done the same for them. You rely on other people to give you information about yourself. You may not agree with their assessment of you, but seeing yourself in the eyes of another person tells you a lot. It tells you many things about them. It may tell you things you didn't know about yourself. And it tells you about how you relate to the people around you.

A clear reflection is one that comes with no prejudice or judgment. When you see yourself reflected in

The Actor

the eyes of someone who truly loves you, you are inspired to be more generous with your love. You're inspired to love yourself more. Good reflections and positive feedback encourage you to be the best artist you can be. In fact, mirror-reflections may be the most fascinating part of the human dream. Let's take a look at the mysteries of mirroring.

Seeing the Mirrored Path

Every lifetime is a solitary experience, no matter how many companions come and go. Let's imagine the maze again. You're alone as you march through the maze, but yours is not the only path. The entire world is a maze. Within that maze, everyone is following his own course. Within the same world, we live in separate realities, but our realities parallel each other and affect each other's lives.

Your parents took a journey of their own, making different choices for different reasons. Your brothers, sisters, and childhood friends chose their own course. All your teachers followed different trajectories toward the finish line. Their journeys, like yours, were mapped out by the people who taught them. Sure, someone else drew their version of the map, but between the entrance and the exit, they improvised. They blazed their own course. You did, too, and will continue to do so, as long as your journey lasts.

And how long is that? Some lives last almost a century, some longer. Some lives are brief. While most of us are still zigzagging through the maze, some dear friends have already left it. Every life is about solving mysteries, and there are countless ways to do that. Where our attention is pulled, we go. Where emotions lead us, we run. We move in directions that suit our interests and curiosities, with companions to assist us in the journey.

Everyone you encounter has an image of you. Everyone reflects that image back to you. Every person is a mirror, in other words. The corridors of your maze are lined with mirrors. Looking at your life this way, you can see the kinds of people that have attracted you, and maybe you can see why you are drawn to some mirror reflections and repelled by others. Looking closely at your friendships and affairs, you can see patterns you didn't recognize until now.

I'm sure you're familiar with garden mazes. They're giant outdoor puzzles where tall hedgerows conceal a system of crisscrossing paths. It's easy to get lost inside a garden maze, but that's part of the thrill. Walking with a sweetheart you can get happily and conveniently lost. You can linger, hide from the world, and enjoy some quiet time together. All the paths eventually lead to an exit, but once inside, it's impossible to tell where that exit might be.

Well, imagine mirrors lining your maze instead of bushes and trees. You are wandering through a world that shows you assorted images of yourself. Wherever you go, you meet a new reflection. You, too, are a mirror for every person you meet. The thing is, you can't accurately reflect yourself. You can never really see yourself in action, so you rely on others to reflect you. And they do.

People see you through their own lens. Their opinions of you are in keeping with their assumptions and expectations. Since you already have an image of yourself set firmly in your mind, any reflection that contradicts that image will seem surprising, even disturbing, to you. Some reflections don't seem to represent you at all.

When life is such a hall of mirrors, which mirrors can you rely on to tell you the truth? Or, more to the point, why should you rely on any of them? Why should another person's opinion of you be so important?

We all want someone to confirm the best image of ourselves, but people are quick to judge. They get a feeling about you right away. They can decide who you are even before meeting you. It's a rare person who looks, listens, and really sees someone. If they love what they see in you, you've found a great mirror. And it works both ways: When you show respect and admiration for someone else, they're naturally drawn to you. They want to see that reflection again and again.

It should be the instinct of a parent to love wholeheartedly, but it sometimes happens that children have to wait to find genuine love later in life. They have to wait to be appreciated by someone who has no preconceptions or expectations—someone who admires them for what they are.

Ultimately, it's up to each of us to love ourselves as we are. It's up to me, and it's up to you. The love and respect you have for yourself determines how others see themselves through you. So let's talk more about that. Let's see how you can create a high standard of art through clear and positive mirroring.

Alice in the Mirror

Professional artists mirror the human condition. They mimic life. They reflect society. We amateurs do much the same. We mirror popular thinking. We mirror contemporary trends. We mirror each other, through our fashion choices and our ideologies. So it's easy to understand how reflections get muddled and distorted.

How we reflect each other affects the quality of our work as artists. It affects our relationships and the way we live our lives. Are you aware of the kind of mirroring that attracts you to someone? You're not always drawn to someone who's kind or forgiving, for example. Maybe you gravitate toward people who are critical and occasionally cruel. Maybe you feel more comfortable being bullied than pampered. You may feel you deserve a tyrant in your life instead of a collaborator.

Then again, you may crave such a perfect reflection that you constantly misrepresent yourself. Some of us want affection above all, even if it means pretending to be something we're not. If you only see your worth through another person's eyes, you might be convinced you can't live without that person. You may never discover yourself at all.

On the other hand, if you gave yourself the love you crave, you wouldn't be so desperate to find it somewhere else. If you respected yourself absolutely, you'd be immune to manipulation. How far would you stray for a few crumbs of affection? What would you do, even now, for a little praise?

How many times have you underestimated your value in order to fit in, or to attract followers? Only you can answer questions like these. No one else can solve the mystery of *you*. No one else can feed your deepest needs. As you've noticed, other mirrors have needs of their own.

Maybe you're aware that some mirrors have a stronger will than you. Some pull you into their world so completely that you care about nothing else. You become more concerned about their drama than your own. You treat them as the main character of your story. You try to live their life. Like the mythical Alice, you're lured into an attractive mirror, you're transfixed, and could remain there indefinitely.

There's a chance you've done this already, you've tried to take another person's journey. You've adopted someone else's habits and celebrated their best memories. You've mirrored their interests and activities.

Eventually it all feels wrong, you find yourself doing things you don't want to do. Your infatuation with some mirrors can lead to obsession, and obsession takes you on a winding path to nowhere.

By "nowhere" I mean self-destruction, or the destruction of a dream. All artists want to feel inspired, yes, but inspiration leads to creativity, where obsession does not. Obsession will likely undo your creation. You need to step back once in a while and see where you are. See where your attention has pulled you. Is it where you want to be, or are you now dedicated to one thing at the expense of all others?

I suggest you use perspective. See as an artist sees. Recognize beauty in yourself, and do everything you can to express it. Great art doesn't have to be more complicated than that. You've probably heard some artists claim they have to suffer to create. Many legendary artists endured poverty and rejection, so suffering is assumed to be an indispensable part of the creative process.

Suffering is a recurring theme in most people's stories, in fact. We're all a little addicted to it, and we have endless excuses. We deserve to suffer, we say. We suffer when we're misunderstood. We suffer for a cause.

We suffer for noble reasons. We suffer for love. We suffer for art.

"Great art requires great suffering" is a universal assumption, but why should it be true? There is real suffering in the world, yes. Physical pain and deprivation exists. Most people struggle to support themselves and their families. They struggle to secure their futures, to find shelter or employment. Others struggle to make sense out of mystery. Struggle is familiar to everyone, but it's not an excuse to suffer.

Every entrepreneur has to fight to make a business work. Painters, poets, musicians, and actors struggle to be recognized, enduring punishing conditions in the process. Dancers and athletes feel the pain of injury and failure. They're not alone in their creative frustration. You feel it too, but telling yourself a story about how much you're suffering does nothing to end the frustration. You, the artist, are responsible for the stories you tell and the mood you set. You're responsible for your happiness, and for your own artistic fulfillment.

Take creative action as a remedy for frustration. Tell a better story. Be attentive to your body, the instrument of your art, and do what you can to heal a mind at war with itself. See clearly and love generously while you stroll through this mirrored maze.

Reflections on Love

Most artists dare to reveal themselves to other people. Do you? Can you step into the bright lights with (or without) the fear of rejection? Do you trust life not to judge you or desert you? Keep in mind that people make judgments, life does not.

It's possible to look into a defective mirror and remain confident. Being reflected poorly doesn't have to result in discouragement. No mirror gives you the whole picture, or the true picture. Every mirror tells you something, however.

You may get mad at someone for failing to see the best in you. You may get defensive, but there's something to be learned from a bad mirror too. Clear, cloudy, or corrupt, all reflections inform you. The more information you have, the better you see. Be skeptical about the information you get, but listen anyway. Listen without judgment and learn.

Without mirrors, you and I would be like most other animals. We would lack the information we need to evolve. We'd miss important revelations even from the poorest reflections. At the same time, we are more than any mirror can show us. We are more than what we see and think. Everything changes when we're willing to explore the mysterious truth of us.

This is where love enters the scene. Far from being blind, love perceives the truth. You understood that in your infancy, and you can relearn it now. There are people in your life who need the brightest reflection you can give. Instead of showing your disappointment, show your admiration. Affirm. Applaud. Do this, and not just for the people you love most. Every person deserves a clear reflection from someone motivated by love.

Your journey through the maze goes on. It twists and bends, providing countless mirror-images along the way. How you respond to the reflections you see depends on how you love yourself—and how fearless you are about loving others, however they may reflect you.

As babies, most of us gazed into clear, bright mirrors. Mommy's smile told us we were precious, Daddy's strength told us we were safe. Everyone reflected a wonderful image back to us. Summer winds carried all the wonders of life to our senses. We were all children once, looking wide-eyed into the mirror, but over the years we started to focus on the distortions. In time, we fell out of love with ourselves. We began to doubt we were capable of loving at all.

When you look in a mirror, you probably only see what you hope to see, expect to see, or most dislike seeing. You see other people the same way. Is that actually seeing? Most of us are hardly aware of what's going on until life wakes us up with a shock. Meanwhile, we're blind to the beauty and unprepared for the truth.

Reflections are not the thing they reflect. The truth of you was never in the glass. *Your warm body is the truth.* I think you realize this now. You are a living, breathing human. You are real, but the realness of you is lost in the reflection. If you've forgotten this, take a few minutes to remind yourself. Sit in front of a full-length mirror. See the whole picture—you, the room, all those colors and shapes—as a visual reproduction of what is real. Everything is visible to you because light is touching the glass, but none of it exists in the glass.

Close your eyes and feel the truth. Feel you, the one who is being reflected. Feel life pushing through your veins. Feel your breath and your heartbeat. Feel the heat of you, and the electric current that runs through your body. You are life.

Life keeps making more life. It does this with no self-importance and no personal stories. You can do the same. You can exist without your stories. You can be true to yourself without explanations or excuses. You can love without conditions and without a doubt.

Don't stand still waiting for someone to prompt you. Put your will into action. Keep turning corners. Keep discovering and growing. Lay the foundations for something new. Your time in the maze is magical, you only have to open your eyes and *see it*.

Why Does Any of This Matter?

Why does it help to see your life as a maze of avenues and alleyways? Your future is determined by the choices you make—to turn right or left, or continue straight ahead. You may also choose to hang out a while, or possibly backtrack. It's interesting to see how those choices were made in the past. It helps to see how they brought you to this place, on this day. It's important to see how you can move forward from here, now that you're aware of your motivations and are willing to modify them.

Let in some light. Light reflects images from one person to another and back again. By recognizing mirrors for what they are, you can respond to them more sensibly. We're talking about human beings, so behind the "glass" is a mind. A mind tends to scramble information. It comes to conclusions, it guesses and assumes. And assumptions, as you know, complicate everything.

Awareness is the ability to see objectively, without making judgements or assumptions. Every mind warps the truth a little, so don't take opinions so personally. When you assess your own behavior fairly, you can be more gracious in your assessment of others. Actors study their characters objectively, fairly. This is how you can study yourself. This is how you can nurture your authentic qualities.

Think about the stage you've set. Maybe it could use some design changes. This isn't about deciding where the furniture goes, I'm talking about the mood. I'm asking whether you're designing a heaven for yourself, or a hell. Heaven. Hell. Let's take some time to understand the difference.

Heaven is a state of mind, of course. When we create a reality where respect rules our behavior, we're in heaven. I respect those close to me. I respect everyone I encounter—and I respect you, without having to know you personally. Let's say you respect me and everyone else in your story. Things go smoothly between us, because we share respect without having to agree on everything. That's heaven.

Hell is something else. Fear rules hell. Life can be intolerable when fear is allowed to set the mood. If respect isn't our natural impulse, we will judge each other. We will accuse each other and fear each other. Heaven and hell are metaphors, but the misery we make is not. A living hell is a real experience. Respect is how we avoid its agonies.

Respect yourself, and let that respect shine out to the world. Let it touch everything you touch and be mirrored back to you. Be aware of how respect transforms your reality. With that kind of awareness comes evolution. How are you evolving? Well, you're daring to see what you couldn't see before. You're opening up to the light's information. You're getting closer to reflecting the truth, and the truth places you in heaven, even as you walk this earth.

What Else Can I Do?

The tension of not knowing what's next, or whether you'll ever be wanted again, exists for all artists. We never feel we've done enough, won enough, or impressed enough people. The worry is always, could I have done more or can I do more?

You're another kind of student now. In this particular school, you're exploring deeper mysteries. You have an appetite for truth. You aspire to be a clear mirror. I urge you to ask questions. Weigh the answers carefully. Hear all sides to a story before you share your opinions, and respect all points of view. Maybe you considered yourself life's victim once, now you are life's accomplice.

And how does that collaboration begin? We conspire with life when we are aware, and when we are adaptable to its changes. We're in cahoots with life when we're open to new information, not closed and defended. We're in partnership with life when we're honest with ourselves. By denying the obvious, we're likely to face consequences. When we lie to ourselves, we'll soon feel the pain.

In the theologian sense, to be impeccable means to be without sin. For you, the artist, it's a sin to go against yourself. It's a sin to disrespect your art. Imagine yourself as impeccable—how would that look and sound? How would you move through the world?

Well, imagine saying what you mean and doing what you say. Imagine you're someone who never assumes, but asks and then evaluates. Imagine that you can listen to criticism without reacting defensively. Imagine doing your best, and that your best efforts evolve over time. If you can imagine yourself responding like this to ordinary situations, you're ready to put these lessons to use.

1) Be impeccable with your words and actions.
2) Don't take things personally.
3) Don't make assumptions.
4) Do your best in every moment.

These lessons are essential tools for an artist of life. Today is a good day to sharpen your skills. Maybe you don't think you're brave enough, or creative enough, but mastery begins with small attempts. It begins by doing the best you can in the moment. Practice. Rehearse. Make an impassioned commitment to your craft.

Under pressure of any kind, we revert to the smallest definition of ourselves. We fall back on the character who runs away in fear, the one who is victimized, or even the one who bullies. It's important to recognize how specifically you identify yourself with the roles and reactions you once relied on. It's important to see, and to be willing to change.

Now is not the time to revert to the smallness of you. Now is the time to step into the light, see what you do, and reshape it. Observe how your emotions rise to support an old story. Shift the emotion, alter the narrative. Laugh. Breathe. Thank life for reminding you that you're more than anyone's definition of you.

Day 5:
The Final
Curtain

"We have a direct sense of life. When you gain that, you will put aside your mirrors and statues, your toys and your dolls."

–George Bernard Shaw

It's no secret that everyone wants to know a secret. We're all diving for answers in an ocean of mystery. More than anything, we want to know who we are—and yet this is the question we're most afraid to ask.

Who am I? you may have asked yourself on occasion. Well, you know what you're not. You're not the roles you play. You're not your reputation and you're not your reviews. You may have always measured your worth in praise. You've faked it. You've overacted. You loved the show, but whenever you had a chance to step away from the stage, you were relieved, weren't you? The drama seemed a little too intense. It looked a little crazy. It felt unnatural.

Most of your behavior may seem over-the-top when you see it from another perspective. Sketch your history on paper, and you can see how playing a role brought you to a crisis point again and again. You can recall the times you lost yourself completely, or when you let down your team. Look carefully. Maybe you assumed too much and miscalculated. You went against yourself often, but there were also times when you preserved your integrity. There were times when you were awesome.

Let your senses feel what you can't explain. Appearances deceive. You appear to be many things at once. You come across as wide range of self-imposed limitations and outrageous possibilities. It seems, above all, that you are your own best kept secret. The truth is much simpler than any of that, as you've discovered this week.

You want to understand the mystery, but you're afraid to look too closely. *What is real?* you wonder. You worry that you've put too much faith in things that are not real. Reality is your mystery to solve. Questions need to be asked and explored. Obstacles need to be faced and conquered. More mysteries are waiting in the wings.

There's more to discover about love, for instance. *What is love?* People often ask. You asked, listened, and shifted your perspective on love—and found that love is more than you imagined. Far from being one whimsical emotion, love is the totality of all emotions.

Far from being a weakness, love is the energy that made you possible—and still drives you to evolve.

Every generation finds new answers to age-old questions. Some generations rediscover answers that were lost and forgotten. Solving one mystery opens the door to many, many more. Pull back the curtain and flood the dark places with light, until you come to the final mystery, which lies beyond the maze.

Leaving the Stage

You may never have thought of your world as a stage before. You may never have considered your actions and reactions as a performance. Having that awareness, however, makes it possible to choose your roles and to play them with intention. Being aware gives you choices. You can choose the times you don't need to play a role at all.

Instead, you can be present and spontaneous. You can make the choice to listen, to observe, and put your attention on what's happening around you. And, maybe for the first time, you can examine the qualities that make you authentic. Your choices change with every situation, but awareness keeps you true to yourself.

Some day you will leave the stage. We all do. The lights will go out and the play will be over. In professional acting, the theater must go dark at some point and actors must fall out of character. They must say goodbye to the troupe and move on. The curtain will come down, and everyone—cast, crew, and happy patrons—will walk out of the theater to resume their lives.

Closings happen many times within one lifespan, just as they do in the theater. Every show begins with great enthusiasm but inevitably comes to an end. Old sets are broken apart, props are put away, and costumes are discarded. How do you prepare to exit the stage for good? How do you ready yourself for the larger mystery beyond the maze?

First, you want to wake from the dream—yes, the dream. A stage play is a dream created by actors. A journey, too, is like a dream. It challenges you to improvise, and to learn different ways of doing things. Your life is a dream that often seems nonsensical. Good luck may run out, and your friends may fail you. Your fortunes rise and fall again. On occasion, tragic events force you to be the hero of your own story.

Maybe you're great at this already. Maybe you consider yourself an accomplished dreamer. Upheavals don't bother you. You're flexible, you're fearless in the face of change. You've done your best in all situations, and your body of work is admirable. Maybe now you can see your life in ways you never could before.

For instance, you are here, actively engaged in your story, and at the same time you're observing the action from a distance. You've learned the art of perspective, as a painter must. You've disciplined yourself to see the whole picture, and to avoid getting lost in the details. You can see life in its totality, but you can also see yourself while you're immersed in the performance.

You're right, your perspective has changed. And maybe you're less attached to the roles you play. But before the lights go out on this amazing show, give yourself one last challenge as an artist: to leave the maze, using your imagination. Just as imagination took you into other worlds back in those early days of childhood, your grown-up imagination can lift you out of the maze while you still occupy it.

While your curiosity is sharp and your will is strong, continue to expand your awareness. Appreciate the value of your losses and successes, and learn to trust future outcomes. As you know, when death happens you will cease to be part of the human experience. It matters that you live it now, with eyes that are open and a mind that is willing to play.

Being human is a wild ride. It's never just one experience. Intensities change. Devotions change. It can be terrifying and exhausting. It can be, and often is, sweetly astonishing. I urge you to see the human experience in its entirety. I encourage you to enjoy the fullness of that experience, while you live—and to face one last obstacle, when you're ready.

The Last Judgment

You're free to be authentic when you no longer fear the judgments of other people. And what about your own judgments? Chances are that you judge yourself even more harshly than you do anyone else. You will continue to do so, until you overcome the temptation to judge at all.

Someday you'll stop. You'll make your final judgment. You'll hear it and cringe at the sound. Every impulse to judge after that will feel alien and uncomfortable. It matters that you pay attention. It matters that you modify your stories inwardly so that you can communicate respect outwardly. It matters to you. It matters to the physical body you occupy, and the people who look to you for guidance.

In order to play a role faithfully, actors assume specific points of view. Characters in a play are supposed to have lived real lives, with past histories to explain their actions. An actor's job is to understand their sensitivities and secret fears—and their tendency to judge.

Imagine if a character had no judgments about anything. Would he seem boring, and unworthy of an audience's attention? Maybe. Most people would say that flawed characters are the most intriguing. Villains are compelling characters, for instance. Perpetual victims are also compelling. It's usually the best and the worst of people that make audiences take notice. But you and I aren't trying to keep audiences entertained anymore, are we?

How would you behave if you no longer needed to please an audience? What if you weren't afraid of being judged? You'd listen better, wouldn't you? You'd relax and observe. You'd delay your reactions and focus on the moment. The entire tone of your performance would change.

Judgment is the villain in your private movie. Once it's driven from the plot, you can explore a vast range of human emotion without all the drama. You can feel without having to make the audience feel. Nobody has to laugh or to cry. No one needs to go home unsettled or depressed. Your name doesn't have to go down in the books as "the greatest performer who ever lived." You can be remembered as someone even more captivating: someone who was authentic.

Professional acting sometimes succeeds where our best efforts as amateurs cannot. Actors often manage to capture moments of truth. Professionals are concerned with making a good living, of course, but also with the integrity of their work. They want to feel proud when their work is done. They want to be elevated by their art. Like many of us, they want to touch a godly truth.

The trouble is, we've been encouraged to focus on our failures. We're distracted by our flaws. As actors-in-training, we were judged on our appearance. We were judged on our manners. It mattered that we performed well in school and behaved well in society. We endured a lot of criticism, so naturally we grew up to focus on our imperfections.

In my view, everything is perfect as it is. You want to develop rather than remake yourself. You've become blind to the wonder of you. Keep in mind that an artist doesn't see imperfection. Artists are beguiled by their subjects. Artists are captivated by the magic of life.

Let's go back to the movies for a minute. Imagine that you're in that dark theater, your arms wrapped around a tub of popcorn. You're ready to be transported. The movie begins. Right away, you're dazzled by the images in front of you. You're quickly caught up in the plot.

Now, imagine that there's a speck of dirt on the screen. Once you've seen it, you can't see anything else. It annoys you, and you can't let it go. You can't focus on the actors or the scenery. Gradually, you lose track of the plot and your emotional connection to the story is lost. The whole point of going to the movies was to enjoy a break from your obsessions—and now here you are, obsessing. More than that, you're missing the wonder. You are missing the magic.

Somewhere, beyond your sight, a light is shining through a strip of celluloid. Or through a prism. Or onto tiny mirrors. Film technology changes and evolves, but the principle is the same: light touches matter, light is reflected, and light's information is dispersed.

In the case of a movie, a series of images is enhanced and then projected onto a screen. You see the result, and you recognize it as a picture story. As you watch, the story becomes your reality, and you respond to it emotionally. The more you believe you're part of the action on screen, the more emotionally invested you get.

It took remarkable genius to put all those elements together to such powerful effect, but it's a perfect example of art duplicating life's mystery. Light shines on matter. Light bounces off matter. What we see triggers certain feelings. Life is an awesome light show, and each of us experiences the show differently.

Fixating on that speck of dust on the screen is a choice. You will focus on it until you decide to broaden your vision and absorb the entire experience. Meanwhile, truth is flashing behind the lens. Life is waiting, calling. Never mind what everyone else is doing. Can you feel it? Are you paying attention?

Life makes all things possible. You make things possible in your own way by creating things out of pure imagination. Inspiration, that mysterious force, allows you to create beauty in infinite ways. It allows you to spark inspiration in others and share a love for what you do.

Humanity can be your playground, or it can be your best excuse to suffer. The world is caught up in its own drama and is paying no attention to yours. Your family taught you to conform, now you can break some of those rules. You can ask impossible questions and face difficult answers. You can find excellence, with or without an audience, and decide for yourself what the next act will bring.

The Next Phase

Acting requires belief and commitment. Being a good audience requires the same thing. When actors can't persuade an audience to believe, they fail at their craft. If the audience isn't willing to accept the premise of a story, however fantastic, they fail as collaborators. What if this happy conspiracy was motivated by a mutual desire for truth?

An entertaining lie is great for the theater, but it doesn't serve us well in ordinary life. Deception is hard to justify or defend. Melodrama can be exhausting. In a play or a movie, it's thrilling to imagine witches stealing children, or alien creatures invading our galaxy. It can be fun to believe superheroes patrol the skies—but we don't want to live in a world that runs on fear or fantasy.

Evolution is about growth. It's about adaptability, and you have the capacity to adapt. You can self-reflect.

You can face irrational fears and dispel them. You can imagine fantastic things without putting your faith in them. You can admit you're dreaming, and you can shift the dream. You can even transform the dreamer.

You've envisioned your path as a walk through a college campus, a place where mysteries are discussed and explored. Life on campus is easy. Your fellow students are there to confide in you, to guide you, and get you where you're meant to be. The idea of Earth as a university campus is illuminating. It reminds you that you're here to learn.

You've also imagined your journey taking place on a stage. Any stage is intimidating, perhaps, but your fears are shared by other players. You've always been an actor, studying at the same drama school as the rest of humanity. You see that your performance skills were taught by experts. You can decide now where those skills will take you.

Finally, I've asked you to see your life as a maze— the kind of place where your progress is hard to measure and where your vision is limited. In a maze, you live with the stress of not knowing where you are or where you're going. A maze is full of false starts and random disappointments. You're surrounded by reflections, but you can't trust them to tell you the truth. So it makes sense to nurture a deep love for yourself. Love is essential to appreciating the beauty of this, your only lifetime.

The idea of walking through a maze is exactly that: an idea. New ideas can help you move beyond your present ways of thinking. This particular idea helps you see how you've walked through life, and how you can move ahead with enthusiasm. Sometimes you've been clueless, sometimes not. You've been paralyzed with fear, and you've also been brave through the traumas. The idea of a maze reminds you that you came into the world *here*, and will exit somewhere over *there*. It's up to you to navigate the spaces in between.

I've asked you to imagine your journey through life in several ways—as a campus, a stage, and a rambling garden maze. Each one paints a picture of your life. Each one places you at a different level of awareness at different points in time. Right now, you may think of yourself as a constant student, never quite ready to rise to the next level. Or you may think you know it all. You may think you graduated long ago.

Maybe you've already taken your show on the road and toured the world. You've built a career on the strength of one role, one winning performance. Of course today you're not what you were yesterday. You're a struggling student one moment, a valedictorian the next. Your audience is with you one day, and they don't show up the next. We're experts and amateurs—in turns, and all at once.

At any point, you can decide if your actions are in sync with your awareness. Your journey will end at the time of your death, but while you live, see things as they are. Enjoy the reflections, but value what is real. The exit to this labyrinth may suddenly appear beyond the next tree or shrub. The end of the journey may come before you've fully appreciated its beauty. While you're here, make sure your eyes are open and your senses are wide awake.

What Can I Do Now?

Take a deep breath. Exercise your imagination and expand your understanding. Focus your energy. First, believe who you think you are. This should require no effort, since that is exactly what you do all the time.

Once you have that familiar sense of comfort—knowing what you know about yourself—stop knowing it. That's right, stop believing. You are not who you think you are. Feel the emotional discomfort of that, and relax into it. Feel safe, not knowing.

Now, feel the sensation of believing something you know to be true about someone close to you. Once again, this is something you do on a constant basis. You think you know people. Once you have that sensation, that absolute conviction that a person is completely known to you, then stop. Stop believing what you think about them is true. Feel a lightness where that belief once existed.

Play with beliefs that way. Recognize a conviction, and then invest belief in an opposing conviction. Finally, discard all conviction on the subject. This leaves you with uncluttered perception moment to moment. The exercise isn't meant to make you stop caring, but to show you how emotionally connected you are to your beliefs. In this way, you see how detachment is possible, and that attaching again is a choice. Believe it is. Believe it is not. As we've discussed, your attention determines what you believe, not the other way around.

Spiritual mastery is about transcending the main character of your story. It's about seeing beyond your immediate environment and expanding your sense of reality. Mastery for a professional artist means the same. Professionals lose themselves in their art. They document what they see and imagine what they cannot see. At their best, they awaken other artists like you and me. They make us aware of things we hadn't yet considered. And awareness grows over time.

Awareness begins in the womb, as the fetus grows and the infant brain develops. There, as matter slowly takes shape, the senses stir, perceiving light and sound, warmth and weightlessness. From those earliest stages, we're all collaborators in our own transformation. Life gives us the raw materials, and we develop them at our own pace.

You've already succeeded at three important challenges: 1) You continue to grow in awareness. 2) You keep evolving, both physically and spiritually. 3) Your will is strengthening. Remember that your will makes change possible, it has the power to discourage you and it has the power to push you beyond normal boundaries of perception.

Awareness. Transformation. Will. Today, and for all future days, these are important tools for your evolution. And you have others. Imagination, for instance, takes you anywhere you want to go. Collaboration intensifies creativity, so don't forget the troupe. You share this vast stage with countless others. Allow them free expression. Respect their talents. Respect invites opportunities—in life and in art.

Every teacher is a guide, offering clues to seemingly unsolvable mysteries. A teacher can point you in the direction of truth, but where the journey will take you is its own kind of mystery. I appreciate your will to wonder and to learn and I've been honored to help you in that effort.

This week, you've seen your life from different perspectives. Whether you imagine yourself walking across a campus or across the world, you've learned from the choices you've made. You've learned from the places you visited and the people who fascinated you.

You've discovered skills you may not have thought you possessed. You've learned to appreciate talents that were developed in childhood and refined as you matured. You've seen how those talents can be shaped to suit your present awareness. You also know that they can be modified or replaced. Instead of acting— acting! acting!—you may choose to settle into the realness of you. You may choose to know yourself as the one warm body in a roomful of mirrors.

You are an authentic being, however you shape your acting skills and however much you crave an audience. Play with life. Play with your fellow artists. Take advantage of every opportunity to learn more about the mystery of you.

Well, I see it's getting late. You and I must leave each other, but only for now. You have my love and my encouragement. If awareness is important to you, the adventure is on. If truth is what you're looking for, opinions don't matter. You've already distinguished yourself by going your own way.

Continue to make choices the way an artist would, and dare to inspire. You were meant to turn inspiration into something magical, *and offer it back to humanity.* That is your gift as an artist, and your enduring legacy.

Class ends

ABOUT THE AUTHORS

Miguel Angel Ruiz, better known as Don Miguel Ruiz, is a renowned Nagualan master, author of the classic The Four Agreements and the bestseller *The Mastery of Love*, among other books. He was born into a family of healers and was raised in rural Mexico by a healer mother and a Nagual grandfather in the Toltec tradition. Today a spiritual leader followed by millions of people, Don Miguel Ruiz practiced as a surgeon until a near-death experience brought him closer to the traditions of the Toltecs, following in the footsteps of his ancestors. He has dedicated much of his life to sharing the teachings of that ancient civilization to guide the individual to personal freedom.

Barbara Emrys was born in France, the daughter of an American diplomat, and grew up in Europe, Africa, and the West Indies. She worked as an actress and film producer until twenty-five years ago, when she met Don Miguel Ruiz and began her apprenticeship on the path of shamanism. She is currently a teacher of the ancient Toltec arts, as well as one of the closest collaborators of the mythical Mexican shaman, with whom she has co-authored several books.